REVIEWS FROM RESTAURANT OWNERS

"Adam is deeply committed to helping restaurant owners succeed. His passion for the industry and no-nonsense approach provide practical strategies that make a real difference in operations and growth. If you're looking for insights from someone who truly cares, this book is it."

—MIKE BAUSCH, OWNER OF ANDOLINI'S
PIZZERIA (TULSA, OKLAHOMA)

"The system Adam describes in this book drove an additional $2 million in sales for our restaurants. We saw a huge jump in online ordering after we started working with Adam's team. It works."

—RAHUL BHATIA, OWNER OF SAFFRON INDIAN
KITCHEN (AMBLER, PENNSYLVANIA)

"We really wanted to get away from relying on the third-party delivery apps. So when we met Adam and learned about his growth system, we were so excited. It's been huge for our restaurant and really helped us feel in control of our own growth. Our online sales, check size, and Google rankings all went up after we implemented his advice."

—KAREN AND PHILLIP HANG, OWNERS OF SUSHI
ME ROLL'N (WEST COVINA, CALIFORNIA)

"Technology is so important for restaurants today. I love how Adam helps restaurant owners harness the power of tech to grow their businesses. Delivery app fees were crushing our profits, and Adam's marketing strategies helped us build our own customer base, helping us go from a single food truck to more than ten brick-and-mortar locations and counting. He's the real deal."

—MO FARRAJ, OWNER OF TALKIN'
TACOS (MIRAMAR, FLORIDA)

"Adam's system works. We used this system and it generated a 30 percent increase in extra online sales for us. Highly recommended."

—SAID HOFIANI, OWNER OF SAN DIEGO KABOB
SHACK (CHULA VISTA, CALIFORNIA)

"Adam is a constant student in the restaurant world, which allows him to be the best teacher and master at his craft. If you are looking to improve the growth and overall success within the four walls of your restaurant, look no further. Adam has all the tools and an approach that will allow you to gain the vital knowledge for your own successful journey. Dive in..."

—JASSON PARRA, OWNER OF LEMON TREE CO. (BOISE, IDAHO)

"Adam knows restaurant marketing inside and out, and he actually cares. No fluff, no gimmicks—just real strategies that help restaurant owners get more customers, make more money, and keep people coming back."

—MARIO DEL PERO, CO-FOUNDER OF MENDOCINO
FARMS (EL SEGUNDO, CALIFORNIA)

RESTAURANT GROWTH SECRETS

The New Rules of
GROWING YOUR RESTAURANT

Restaurant Growth Secrets

ADAM GUILD

Owner Press

RESTAURANT GROWTH SECRETS

The New Rules of Growing Your Restaurant

FIRST EDITION

ISBN   978-1-5445-4889-0   *Hardcover*
      978-1-5445-4888-3   *Paperback*
      978-1-5445-4887-6   *Ebook*

Cover Design by Rachael Brandenburg

For all the owners, especially my mom.

Contents

Preface

WHAT THIS BOOK IS ABOUT
(AND WHAT IT'S NOT ABOUT)

Hey! My name is Adam Guild.

Before we get started, I wanted to introduce myself and tell you what this book is about and what it's not about.

This book is *not* about getting more social media followers. Yet the secrets I'm going to share with you will help you get more new customers than ever.

This book is *not* about building a marketing team. Yet these secrets will help you use automations and AI to operate as if you had one.

If you're like most restaurant owners, you know your digital presence is important, but you're struggling with getting new customers online. You want a way to get more direct online orders in a way that's predictable, measurable, and repeatable.

You've thought that maybe you need more social media exposure. Or maybe you think you need to build a marketing team or hire a marketing person.

That's rarely the case. The problem is *not* exposure on social media.

The problem is *not* that you need to hire a marketing person.

The problem is that you don't have a system that reliably delivers profitable online sales.

A system is a set of parts that are organized to achieve your goal. Each part of the system works with the other parts to achieve the goal.

You know how each part of a car's engine works with the other parts to power the car?

It's possible to have a system that drives sales for a restaurant.

That system is the thing that most restaurant owners are missing.

Story time.

Five years ago, I saw a restaurant that was driving sales using a reliable and predictable system. The owner had spent ten years and millions of dollars developing his system.

The restaurant owner's name is Kimbal Musk. He started out as a successful tech entrepreneur, co-founding his first company, Zip2, with his brother, Elon Musk. They later sold Zip2 for $300 million. With that money, he did something unusual for a tech guy: he went into the restaurant industry.

Using his tech background, he developed custom software for his restaurants. His restaurants quickly grew to multiple locations and restaurant industry fame.

So, as a tech guy who was building for restaurants, connecting with him was one of my earliest goals. And after trying many different ways, I finally got an introduction.

I was so nervous going into that meeting. My voice was shaking when I met him.

"Most independent restaurant owners don't have millions of dollars to spend on their own technology," I told Kimbal. "But whatever it is that you're doing, others need to be able to do it too. And they need to be able to afford it."

He agreed! He said he was inspired to see a nineteen-year-old who was so passionate about building tech for restaurants, and he invested in my company, Owner.com. Kimbal gave me a full tour of his restaurants, from upscale concepts to takeout-heavy casual places. Even better, he showed me the technology he'd built. He revealed the whole system that was driving sales for his casual restaurant businesses. It blew my mind.

I saw five key components that were driving sales for Kimbal's restaurants:

1. Google (search engine optimization): to drive website traffic
2. Restaurant website: to drive direct orders
3. Direct online ordering: to grow the guest list
4. Guest list (emails and phone numbers): to drive mobile app downloads and repeat orders
5. Mobile app: to grow repeat orders

More importantly, I saw how all five components fit together in the perfect way to drive sales.

I made my first sketch of the Restaurant Growth System:

Restaurant Growth System

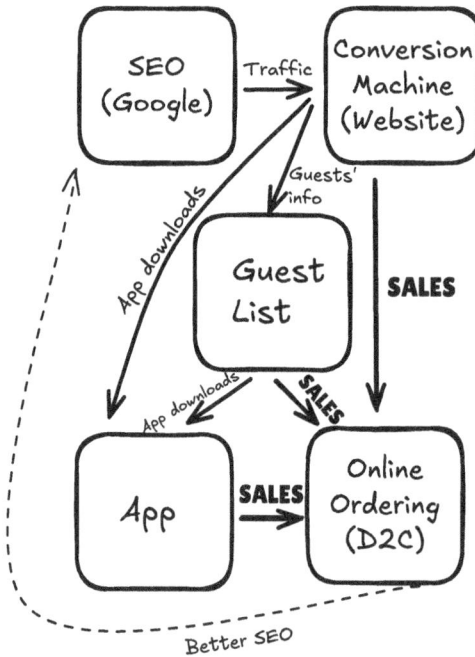

This looks complicated at first, but don't worry! That's why I wrote this book. I will explain each part of this system. You'll see how all the parts work together to grow your restaurant by driving more online takeout and delivery orders.

It all comes down to building the perfect online experience. When most people hear that, they think I'm talking about social media posts. But Kimbal paid very little attention to social media. Instead, he made sure his website worked perfectly with his online ordering and his loyalty program. He built an app that people loved to use. He was never focused on social media. He wasn't trying to make his videos go viral on Instagram. He was focused on making sure all the touchpoints worked together to guide customers through each step of buying—and buying repeatedly. He was optimizing everything around sales, not just looking nice.

What exactly did Kimbal Musk do to make sure his restaurants succeeded? How did he become a restaurant industry superstar almost overnight? And *how can a cash-strapped local restaurant owner do what he did?*

That is what this book is about.

This book will take you on a journey similar to the one Kimbal Musk took me on. It will help you see how to set up your restaurant's website to get more customers. It will help you make more money from the customers you already have. When you start using this growth system, you'll open the floodgates. It will give you more money to invest in growing and improving your business. This book will also help you communicate with your guests in a way that makes them naturally want to buy more from you.

i

When you apply this growth system, you will transform your business. You will get more direct orders—so you won't have to pay as much in crazy fees to delivery apps. You'll get a lot of new guests because you'll know the most effective way to allow more people to find out about your restaurant online. You will get more repeat guests (or "regulars"), and you'll know how to turn one-time customers into regulars. You'll make—and keep—more money. You'll be confident in the future of your restaurant.

And most importantly, the world will be a better place. I know this sounds cheesy, but I believe it in my bones. Nobody wants to live in a world where the only restaurants that succeed are chain restaurants. Not me, not you, not your customers. The world needs your independent restaurant.

That is what this book is about.

Why I Wrote This Book

My restaurant marketing addiction began when I was eighteen years old. I remember the exact night.

It was my mom's birthday. We were at a restaurant to celebrate. Just before she blew out the candles on her birthday cake, she said to my brother and me, "This is the first year in my fifties when I'm really excited about my future again."

Let me explain.

When I was growing up, my mom had a vision for a business. It was a dog-grooming business that would bring our whole neighborhood together around top-notch dog care and great service.

She saved money for years, took out loans against our house, and put all of her life savings on the line to get started.

But she opened on a quiet street. There wasn't a lot of car traffic or foot traffic. So, it was hard for her to attract new customers.

When she did get new customers, they loved the experience. They left feeling energized and cared for. They became regulars and told their friends to visit my mom too.

But still, she couldn't get enough exposure in those early days to make the business profitable.

My mom saw Petco a few blocks away. They had a huge customer base for their grooming service. They were on a significantly busier block. They'd had twenty years to establish their business.

My mom knew she could serve those customers better—if only they knew her!

She was always stressed about losing her business. She had staked so much on it.

She started trying different online growth methods. First, she posted a lot on Instagram and Facebook. Then a salesperson from Yelp contacted her and sold her the $1,000/month package for getting new customers. Then she tried ads. Then she tried direct mail. After six months and more than $10,000 spent, her business still struggled.

At this point, she had only a few months of cash left.

She still had a small base of customers who loved her, but it wasn't enough to survive.

She asked for help from her weird, nerdy seventeen-year-old son, Adam.

She knew I'd started learning how to grow a business through gaming. When I was twelve, I started a *Minecraft* server. (A *Minecraft* server is a game within a game. It's a separate game within *Minecraft* with its own rules and, potentially, its own business model). By the time I was sixteen, more than seven million people were regularly playing *Minecraft* on my server. My customer base was bigger than the population of thirty of the fifty US states!

My mom figured I must have learned something about growth, to go from zero to millions of users with no money.

I agreed to help her, but I didn't know where to start. My experience was only in the online world, in online gaming specifically. I didn't know how I could actually get people in the real world to visit my mom's dog-grooming business.

So I started experimenting.

Initially, I thought the answer was social media because that was a major way my younger brother and I had grown our *Minecraft* servers. We had a ton of experience with social media, so we built up a big following for her. We grew her Instagram audience to more than ten thousand followers, and we got thousands of likes on her Facebook page within a few weeks.

But even though she was gaining a lot of traction on social media, it wasn't translating into sales.

We were getting desperate.

We had just a few months of cash left before her business would have to close.

And, for a shocking reason that I would discover later, the tactics that worked in the gaming industry weren't working for my mom's local business.

So we tested a different idea: instead of social media, we focused on helping her rank at the top of the Google results for dog grooming in West Hollywood.

It was one of the twenty things we tried—and, thank God, it worked!

Once she started appearing at the top of Google's local search results, she got a steady stream of new customers. They were excited to find her business because they had been searching for dog-grooming services.

Over the next six months, I saw my mom's life change completely.

At first, she was struggling, stressed about money, and terrified about potentially losing her business or our house.

Then she finally had the right system to succeed online. I saw her regain excitement about her future. She had so much pride in what she'd built.

Fast-forward seven years, and my mom is running a million-dollar dog-grooming business. Over the years, the same foundations we created at the outset have continued to bring her more customers—thousands of them.

At the beginning of that process, when I saw my mom's life change, I realized that this was my calling.

I needed to find a way to build a business and a life around helping people like her. I knew there were others. My mom wasn't the only person who was improving life in her community with a business that people loved—if they could discover it. She wasn't the only person who had brought something magical into the world and who just needed the right tools to succeed online.

There are millions of small business owners in similar situations.

Independent restaurant owners are a big part of that group.

If you're reading this, you're probably an independent restaurant owner. You worked your way up. You formed ideas about how to create a restaurant of your own, and you finally saved money and started one. You might want to expand to many locations one day, or not. You might not want to scale—but you still want to survive and thrive as the world continues to move online. That means you need to compete with national chains.

Competing with those chains means knowing how to use online platforms to drive revenue and great guest experiences.

But those big chains have resources that you don't. They've spent years and millions of dollars on technology for their business—time and money that you don't have.

That's why I'm here.

I'm obsessed with the idea of understanding the systems that benefit big corporations and giving those systems to people like my mom. I'm obsessed with helping people who are already creating magical experiences and who just need the right system to adapt to the online world.

My mom thought she couldn't compete against Petco, but that wasn't true. She just needed the right system.

Similarly, people think mom-and-pop restaurants can't compete with corporations like Domino's. But that's not true. They, too, need the right system.

One of the biggest barriers for independent restaurant owners is that they've been conditioned to believe three lies.

These lies are killing millions of restaurants—by preventing their owners from getting and using the tools they need to survive and grow.

Lie #1: You need to be active on social media.

Lie #2: You need to use delivery apps, or you'll lose your customer base.

Lie #3: You need a team of tech whizzes and a lot of money to succeed online.

We'll talk about these next.

The Three Lies That Are Killing Independent Restaurants

The number of big companies in the restaurant world keeps growing. Whenever I talk to people, they tell me they keep seeing their favorite local spots replaced by corporate chains.

Everyone hates to see a great local restaurant replaced by an Applebee's. So why does it keep happening? Why do independent restaurants keep getting killed?

After years of studying this trend, I've found out what's going on.

Twenty years ago, it was enough for restaurants to just provide great food and provide great service. Those things alone are hard to do.

When restaurant owners did those two things right, they were guaranteed a huge following of loyal customers. Often they could expand to multiple locations.

But over the past five years, the world has changed. Most of the guest experience is now online. Guests initially discover your restaurant on Google or Yelp. Then they check the reviews, compare them to reviews of other restaurants, and make some fast decisions based on your website. And they order from you by clicking through your online ordering or booking system.

Previously, it would have been rare for a restaurant to have thousands of loyal "regulars" who never set foot in its dining room. Now it's pretty common.

The online experience was once a nice-to-have for tech-savvy guests. Now it has become the primary guest experience. Corporations have caused this change. They've conditioned people to expect an amazing technology experience everywhere. They've spent billions of dollars building their own amazing tech experiences.

Domino's is one of the most obvious examples: they have spent billions of dollars building their own technology, and they run commercials telling people how easy it is to order their food thanks to their technology. We've all seen it: the Domino's delivery guarantee that comes from ordering on their app. They also advertise how you can order via voice or with just a tap.

Of course, you see delivery apps like Grubhub in the mix. They're tech companies that threw massive resources at their apps to make everything super smooth, super convenient, and super fast. They use what they've built to justify charging restaurants ridiculous fees.

Independent restaurants were left behind in this change.

Even worse, when the coronavirus pandemic hit, the changes sped up.

The world suddenly shifted to being entirely off-premises.

This quickly benefited the big corporations in the restaurant industry. More guests became used to a sleek digital experience with restaurants.

This trend has devastated independent restaurant owners. All the numbers show it. The number of independent restaurants is declining every year. But the total number of restaurants is growing.

Corporations are winning.

The big corporations have been the best at providing an amazing technology experience.

Smaller restaurants haven't had the right tools to keep up, let alone succeed, in the digital world.

But things are changing now. My team and I have studied the tools that large corporations have weaponized against independent restaurants. We've learned how these large corporations develop amazing guest experiences that make people want to order from them again and again. We've found that, just like

Kimbal Musk, they rely on systems that work together. We've found the right tools and system for succeeding online.

Independent restaurants can create similar experiences for their customers.

They can now use the weapons that have been used against them for the past ten years.

They can not only survive but also grow—a lot—by using the right tools in the right way.

By using the right tools, you can fuel millions of dollars in sales and fast expansion. That's what is happening in many of the stories you'll read about in this book.

Before we get there, we need to talk about the three big lies that are killing independent restaurants. It's impossible to apply the seven secrets if you're buying into these three lies:

Lie #1: You need to be active on social media.

Lie #2: You need to use delivery apps, or you'll lose your customer base.

Lie #3: You need a team of tech whizzes and a lot of money to succeed online.

Let's tell the truth about each of these.

Social media is the way to grow sales nowadays. Let's get you some IMPRESSIONS and thousands of LIKES! If we assume a 1% conversion rate, that's 10 new customers for every 1,000 impressions!

I guess that sounds like it could be true.

Social Media Consultant

Restaurant Owner

LIE #1: YOU NEED TO BE ACTIVE ON SOCIAL MEDIA

You've probably had this experience:

A young guy approaches you. He says his Instagram service will get you lots of new customers through social media.

You believe him. After all, industry influencers always say that social media is the way to grow a business nowadays. You believe he knows what he's doing. You can see some of his work with other restaurants.

You think, "This is how restaurants grow. I have to invest in it."

You sign a six-month agreement. The guy promises to grow your Instagram followers and bring in new customers.

At first, it's exciting. Your posts get more likes, your profile gains followers, and you think this will soon translate to sales.

At the end of the first month, he reports one thousand new impressions, fifty new followers, and two thousand likes.

You say, "Great, but how much did that drive in sales?"

Dead silence.

Then he might say, "With one thousand impressions, if we assume 1 percent converted into customers, that's ten new customers."

It's possible. But what he's not telling you is that those one thousand impressions happened globally.

One thousand impressions just means one thousand people saw your post.

It doesn't mean they're interested in your post. And it doesn't mean they live near your restaurant.

He keeps telling you about increasing impressions. He keeps selling you social media dreams. But you're not seeing the results in your bank account. You can't pay rent with likes.

Not all of these guys are scammers. Sometimes they don't realize how ineffective their service is for restaurants in particular.

Everyone "knows" that social media is the most powerful tool businesses can use today to grow. There's some truth to that. But it's not true for restaurants.

If you're surprised to hear this, you're not alone. I'm surprised to be saying it!

If anyone should be advocating for social media, it's me.

Before I founded Owner.com, I grew my *Minecraft* server largely through social media. At its peak, it had more than seven million users, and I started with a total budget of forty dollars. I started the server when I was twelve years old. The only person I could afford to hire to help me grow the social media pages was my ten-year-old brother, Topper.

Over the years, Topper became an expert at growing social media pages. He didn't just help with the *Minecraft* server— he also became one of the biggest social media creators in the world. He has more than one hundred million followers across YouTube and TikTok, amounting to billions of views a year. He's created an empire on social media, and I've seen it change his life firsthand.

So I'm not saying social media isn't powerful. It is.

But for restaurants, it's not a powerful tool for getting customers.

Social media doesn't attract many new customers because it reaches a global audience.

When you post a video on Instagram, it's exciting to think that it could get thousands of views and likes. But those views come from all over the world. That's great if you own a *Minecraft* server or a global fashion brand. Then, anyone can buy your product or download your game. It doesn't matter where they are. That's why many businesses use social media to grow.

But the situation is different for restaurants. They only serve customers within about ten miles of their location. Most restaurant customers live within just five miles of the restaurant.

This means that when a video goes viral on social media, it's unlikely to bring in new customers. The chances of the viewers living nearby are very low.

Another point: people use social media for fun, not to find new places to eat. They go on social media to connect with friends, family, and celebrities, not to see restaurant ads.

So when restaurants post about their chicken parmesan special, it's the wrong message at the wrong time. Social media users ignore it. Many studies show that people are skilled at ignoring advertisements, including social media posts from restaurants.

To make matters worse, more than 99 percent of restaurant posts on Instagram aren't shown to people who don't already follow the restaurant. It decides what content to show based on engagement. A celebrity's post will naturally get more likes than a restaurant's post about a special, so Instagram boosts the celebrity's post more and more. Over time, as this keeps happening, fewer and fewer people will see the restaurant's post.

The truth is that you don't need to spend time creating new content for social media every day.

It's good to have a profile with some food photos. But you don't need to sink resources into it.

Many of the most successful restaurants practically ignore social media.

Instead, they make themselves easier to find on Google.

For example, I know a restaurant owner named Mo Farraj. His business, Talkin' Tacos, started with just one location: a food truck.

Over the past four years, he's grown from that single location to ten brick-and-mortar locations. He's now franchising across state lines.

Mo's story is interesting because Mo experimented with two strategies for promoting his business online:

1. Making his business easy to find on Google
2. Using social media

He tried these two strategies at the same time and tested which one led to better results.

Mo invested heavily in Instagram, posting more than ten times a week, curating his profile, and following all the best practices. He had team members dedicated specifically to those tasks. Within three years, he gained more than one hundred thousand followers for his restaurant—which expanded from one location to ten locations in that time.

Mo also made himself easier to find on Google. He made sure that when people searched for a restaurant like his online, Talkin' Tacos was the first that came up. Optimizing his website to be searchable on Google took significantly less money and time than working on his social media presence.

Considering that Talkin' Tacos has more than two hundred thousand followers and thousands of likes on every post, you'd expect social media to be the top driver of Mo's growth.

Where do Mo's customers come from?

Mo's Talkin' Tacos has more than 200,000 followers on social media and thousands of likes on every post. Yet most of Mo's new customers come from Google.

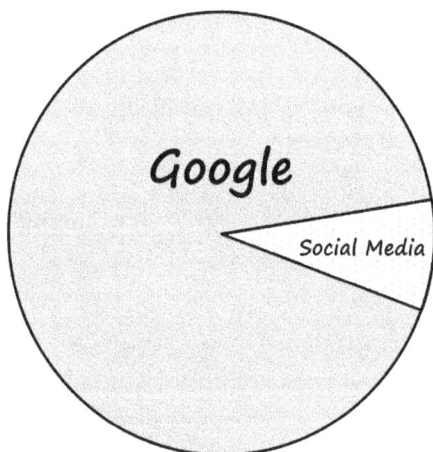

Yet we can track where his customers are coming from. And the data shows that Mo's huge social media following accounts for less than 10 percent of his new customers. Google, on the other hand, represents more than 90 percent.

Mo put much less effort into Google, but it delivered a much higher return. Mo's story shows that making yourself easy to find on Google is a far more effective way of growing your restaurant business than social media is.

By the way, Mo's not the only proof of this truth.

My team has surveyed thousands of restaurants' customers to find out how they heard about the restaurants. We've also tracked thousands of restaurant websites to see if social media was driving new customers.

All the numbers say the same thing.

Across thousands of restaurants, Instagram accounted for less than 5 percent of new customers.

And what about Instagram, Facebook, and TikTok combined?

Less than 10 percent.

So where did the other 90 percent come from?

Mostly from Google, a channel many overlook because they think it's old-school. That's why we're going to discuss Google in more depth when we get to Secret 2: Translate for Mr. Google.

First, let's talk about Lie #2.

LIE #2: YOU NEED TO USE DELIVERY APPS LIKE GRUBHUB OR YOU'LL LOSE CUSTOMERS

Most restaurant owners remember what Grubhub promised, but not what the app ultimately did.

At first, the company promised to bring new customers that the restaurants wouldn't have gotten otherwise. They charged only a 10 percent fee.

This seemed like a good deal to restaurant owners. A lot of them signed up.

But as Grubhub grew, the deal grew worse. They started taking 30 percent of every transaction instead of just 10 percent—even though profit margins in the restaurant industry are usually only 5 percent.

As a result, restaurant owners often lose money on delivery app orders.

Grubhub (and other similar apps) also stopped sharing customer details, such as email addresses.

So restaurants couldn't stay in touch with their customers.

And the terrible secret? Most Grubhub orders aren't from new customers. They're from people who already know and love the restaurant.

Most of the time, delivery apps don't bring new business. They bring a few new customers, but mostly they rely on preexisting relationships.

The app's original promise has been completely broken.

Grubhub and similar companies are stealing customers from restaurants. They then sell these customer relationships back to the restaurants.

The industry has changed. Restaurant owners don't have direct relationships with their customers anymore. They don't even know their customers' names, let alone their email addresses or phone numbers, when orders come through these platforms.

Restaurant owners sense the danger of this.

They even use hostage language to describe what's happening to them.

They tell me, "Delivery apps are holding our customers hostage. They're charging a ransom of 30 percent of the order."

That old promise was broken a long time ago. But now restaurant owners believe that they won't have customers without the delivery apps.

They think these apps are a necessary evil.

They assume that if they stop using these apps, they'll lose their customers.

The truth is that you won't lose your customers if you stop using delivery apps.

You can replace those apps with an online ordering system

that's better for you—as long as it's better for your customers too. You also need to tell them why it's better for them to order directly from you.

If you take the right steps to replace those apps with your own online ordering system, you'll likely give your customers a better experience. This will help you gain their trust and earn more money.

In time, you can become independent of delivery apps. And you can grow your restaurant faster than ever.

Don't believe me?

Let's take a trip to Wichita.

Delivery Apps
Then vs. Now

THEN	NOW
• Charged 10% fee	• Charge **30%** fee
• Shared customer names and email addresses	• **Don't** share customer names and email addresses

Doo-Dah Diner in Wichita is the most popular diner in Kansas.

Timirie, its owner, used to rely heavily on delivery apps like Grubhub. She was paying thousands of dollars in fees every month to these platforms.

She didn't like it, but she saw these apps as necessary evils—things she had to use or else she'd lose customers.

We tried to convince her to replace the apps with her own online ordering system. She was skeptical. In the past, she'd tried Square's online ordering system on her website, but it didn't work. Customers continued to use delivery apps to place their orders.

Still, Timirie decided to take our advice. In twelve months, her online orders grew 6x. She's made hundreds of thousands of dollars. She stopped using delivery apps like Grubhub.

She was surprised to see that her sales didn't go down. They went up because her customers started ordering directly from her app and website. This showed that delivery apps like Grubhub aren't necessary.

Timirie didn't lose her customers. Instead, her customers chose to follow her and stayed loyal to her brand.

Maybe you're thinking, "Adam, it sounds like what you're talking about is going to cost me a lot of money, and I will have to hire a whole team of tech whizzes to compete against big restaurant chains. But we don't have that type of budget."

That leads me to the third lie that's killing restaurants.

LIE #3: YOU NEED A TEAM OF TECH WHIZZES AND A LOT OF MONEY TO SUCCEED ONLINE

This was true once.

In the past, you had to be superhuman to run a business and master every single piece of online marketing.

You'd have to learn how to use multiple tools and measure their success—all while running a restaurant day in and day out.

That was completely impractical.

How are you supposed to get an MBA in marketing while running a restaurant?

Even if you somehow pulled off that heroic feat, you'd still need a team of people. You'd need them to use the online tools necessary to compete with a business like Domino's.

Domino's employs many people who specialize in each marketing tool. They use various software programs to constantly improve the performance of every tool. Being a large corporation, they have the resources to do that.

That's not the case for independent restaurant owners.

All too often, they've had to cobble together fifteen tools on their own. A typical restaurant owner uses Squarespace for their website, Mailchimp for email, Fivestars for loyalty, EZ

Texting for text-message marketing, ezCater for catering, an add-on from their POS for online ordering, and ten other tools.

That becomes an extremely time-consuming process to manage. It isn't practical.

Cobbling Together Tech Tools

Many independent restaurant owners have to cobble together different tech tools—a time-consuming process that isn't practical.

Owners can't spend all day learning and executing every element of digital marketing. They have to run the restaurant.

They were set up to fail.

Because even if they figured out how to use each tool, they would still have to figure out the perfect way to fit the tools together in just the right way to produce sales and growth.

Cobbling these tools together without knowing the Restaurant Growth System is like trying to connect a pile of pistons, valves, shafts, and filters into a car engine without knowing how a car engine is actually supposed to look. The Restaurant Growth System is like the car engine.

Restaurant Growth System

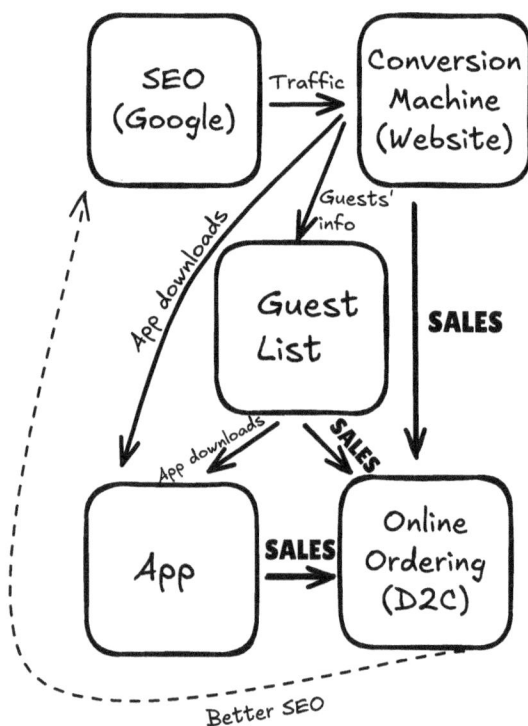

Tools like Mailchimp and ChowNow are like valves and filters. Someone could use those valves and filters to assemble this engine if they knew how the engine was supposed to look.

Now I have two pieces of good news.

- **Good News #1:** By the time you finish this book, you will know how your restaurant's "engine" should look. You'll understand each part of the Restaurant Growth System. You'll also understand how the pieces fit together to achieve the goal of driving sales.
- **Good News #2:** You'll have what you need to build this engine for yourself—but you don't have to. Because of artificial intelligence (AI) and the latest technology, it's now possible for restaurant owners to have one simple tool that provides the growth system for them. It does everything needed to succeed online automatically, without a team.

With the new tool, all you have to do is set up your restaurant once. You upload your menu and some brand assets (like your logo), and the rest is done for you in the background. The tool has proven templates that work. It gives you the ability to reach out to your customers and does everything you need to create an amazing online customer experience. Online marketing doesn't have to be nearly as time-consuming or expensive as it was before.

There are multiple versions of this tool sold by different companies. I built one of them. It's called Owner.com. But this is not an Owner commercial! I want to share this information in such a way that you can apply it to your restaurant even if we never officially work together. The ideas in this book can work with any platform that you're using.

Building Owner is how I came to know so much about this world. I've spent every day for the past seven years obsessed with this world, and my team and I have helped thousands of restaurants with their growth.

The point is that today, you don't need a team of tech whizzes to grow your business. It used to be true that you needed tech specialists to compete online, but it's not true anymore. Now you just need to know exactly what it takes to make a restaurant grow in the online age.

I call these bits of knowledge "secrets" because the big chains and corporations know them, but they don't share what they know. I'm now going to share what they know.

In this book, you will learn:

- how to get discovered online without social media
- how to skyrocket online sales without delivery apps
- how to use technology to your advantage—cheaply and without a team of tech whizzes
- the best ways to get more customers
- how to retain loyal customers
- how to increase the profit of each order
- how to upsell to get more from each customer
- how to build a brand for your restaurant
- how to apply secrets from Domino's and Cava, even if you have no desire to scale to that size

This book is about strategies, not tactics. In it, we focus on helping you master the strategies to grow a restaurant.

But we won't describe step-by-step how to use each piece of technology. Specific technologies and tactics become less relevant over time. But if you master the strategies, you can adapt as technologies change.

Each chapter will teach you strategies. Throughout this book, I share web pages that will lead you to the best free resources to take action on these strategies.

I will update those web pages so this information stays as relevant as possible.

Understand the New Guest Journey

There are only three ways to grow your restaurant:

1. Get more customers.
2. Turn them into repeat customers.
3. Get more profit per order.

The key to doing all of these is to create the perfect customer experience. Creating the perfect customer experience starts with seeing through the eyes of your customers.

You have to know what they need and want. What are they doing and thinking, from the moment they start looking for a restaurant to the moment they walk away?

Three Ways to Grow Your Restaurant

1

Get more customers

2

Turn them into repeat customers

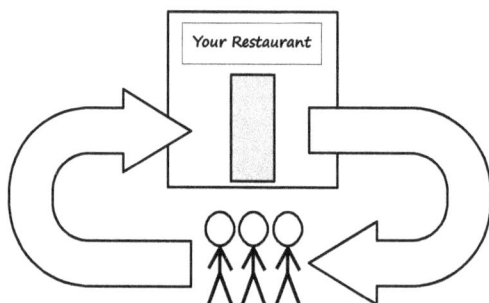

3

Get more profit per order

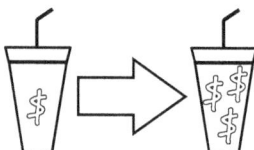

To know these things is to know your customer's journey. Let's look at an example.

A PERFECT CUSTOMER EXPERIENCE

Megan has invited her friend, Rachel, to her house to watch a movie. They're kind of hungry, so they check Megan's fridge. Nothing good for dinner. They decide to order out.

Megan wants to get something they both like: pizza! But she has only recently moved to the neighborhood. She doesn't yet know which nearby pizzeria is best.

So she takes out her phone, opens Google, and types "best pizzeria in Santa Monica."

Google quickly shows her a list of some pizzerias nearby.

Bill's Pizzeria is the first on the list. It grabs her attention because she thinks to herself, "Bill's Pizzeria is showing up first. That must mean that it's the best option and that it has pretty good reviews."

Megan clicks on the link to Bill's Pizzeria, and it takes her to the restaurant's website.

The website experience is critical for Megan. She wants to know what kind of pizza Bill's Pizzeria serves. She knows there are different types of pizza styles. There are some styles of pizza she doesn't like.

On the website, Bill's Pizzeria describes itself as a classic New York–style pizza place. Good news! That's exactly the kind of pizza Megan likes—the kind she used to order from the pizzeria in her old neighborhood.

Now Megan starts wondering whether Bill's also serves calzones. Also, she knows Rachel likes Caesar salad. Does Bill's Pizzeria serve that?

Megan starts exploring the website to find answers.

As she scrolls, she sees images of a calzone and a Caesar salad.

More good news!

But now Megan has another thought: "Is this place actually good?" She's been misled by photos before. She wants to know what people think about this place. Do people love the calzones, or is it just the cheese pizza they rave about?

Megan starts scrolling some more. As though the website read her mind, the next section features reviews.

This section has specific customer comments: not just "I love Bill's Pizzeria," but "I love Bill's Pizzeria because they do calzones better than anyone in Santa Monica. Everything about the calzone is delicious. The crust is perfectly crispy on the outside, and the cheese on the inside is gooey. It reminds me of living in New York when I was in college."

These reviews answer Megan's most important questions.

But she's not done questioning.

Megan has decided that Bill's serves the type of pizza she likes, that Bill's has the dishes she and Rachel want, and that people in the community think highly of Bill's food. But there's still lots to explore on Bill's menu, and the website is perfectly crafted for her new iPhone.

She's had annoying experiences with independent restaurants' websites. She has had to pinch and scroll to see the menu because nothing was formatted to the right size for her phone. Not so with Bill's. As Megan scrolls effortlessly through Bill's menu, she sees delicious-looking pictures of Bill's food. The pizzeria has invested in quality photography. She's starting to eat with her eyes.

She had thought of just ordering a calzone and a Caesar salad, but the meatballs look really good too! She decides to add them to her cart.

But Megan still has to get the items she's placed in her cart, so the next question on her mind is "How do I place my order?"

Normally, she would order through Grubhub. But she sees on Bill's website that she can order from Bill's directly. The website says it's better to order directly from Bill's instead of using Grubhub: it will cost less, she'll get faster service, and she'll start earning loyalty points toward free food.

Megan now has a clear next step. She's decided that she wants pizza. She wants it from Bill's Pizzeria. And she knows that the best way to get what she wants is to order directly from Bill's website to save money, get faster service, and earn free food.

So Megan clicks the "Order Now" button, and it takes her to Bill's online ordering system.

Bill's online ordering system has the same look and feel as the Bill's Pizzeria website. Her experience with the website built her trust in Bill's: she saw the menu, read the reviews, and felt confident enough to place an order.

And now, clicking "Order Now" doesn't take her to a different website. That would feel suspicious and might make her question whether she can trust this ordering site.

Instead, the familiar look and feel of Bill's ordering system maintains her trust. It helps make her more comfortable placing an order and typing in her card details on the website.

Megan proceeds to check out with her Caesar salad, calzone, and meatballs.

The website notices that she hasn't yet added any drinks or desserts. So it suggests, "You might also enjoy..."

The site shows Megan a few popular desserts and drinks. Drinks and desserts sound perfect for a movie! So Megan adds the molten lava cake and the Mexican Coke to her cart.

Just like that, Megan has had a great guest experience. Plus, her order is now twice as profitable for Bill's as it would have been if she'd ordered on Grubhub or another app. That's because the owner made sure to upsell the items that would increase the pizzeria's profit. The food cost for a calzone is pretty high, but the Mexican Coke and molten lava cake have famously low food costs. It's great that Bill's is selling those high-profit items.

Megan reaches the checkout page and feels relieved that it

doesn't ask her to enter a username and password or to create an account—one of the most annoying experiences!

Instead, she sees the option to check out using Apple Pay or Google Pay. In two clicks, she completes her order.

Megan has chosen to have the food delivered. Bill's Pizzeria has driver tracking built into their website, so Megan can see a map of where the driver is.

Now if Rachel asks when they're going to eat, Megan can open the tracking map and give Rachel a time estimate.

The tracking system makes Rachel feel that Bill's Pizzeria is honest and trustworthy. It confirms her sense that she's picked the right place. It's also good for Bill's that Megan isn't calling the restaurant to ask where her food is.

When Megan receives the food from Bill's, she notices that the driver is polite and on time.

The food arrives in a nice bag that says "Bill's Pizzeria: A Taste of New York in Santa Monica."

The branding fits what she was looking for. It reinforces her feeling that she picked the right place.

When Megan tries the pizza, she falls in love with the food. She's found her new go-to pizza place! Over the next ten years, Megan places $50 orders twice per month, spending $12,000 at Bill's Pizzeria because the owner nailed the guest experience.

Megan's story is the story of a perfect customer experience. Bill's Pizzeria understood the customer's journey and carefully crafted the customer's experience every step of the way.

But the situation didn't have to go so well for Megan and Bill's Pizzeria.

At any point along Megan's journey, Bill's Pizzeria might have failed to provide Megan with a good customer experience.

Let's talk about some of the pitfalls that could have ruined everything.

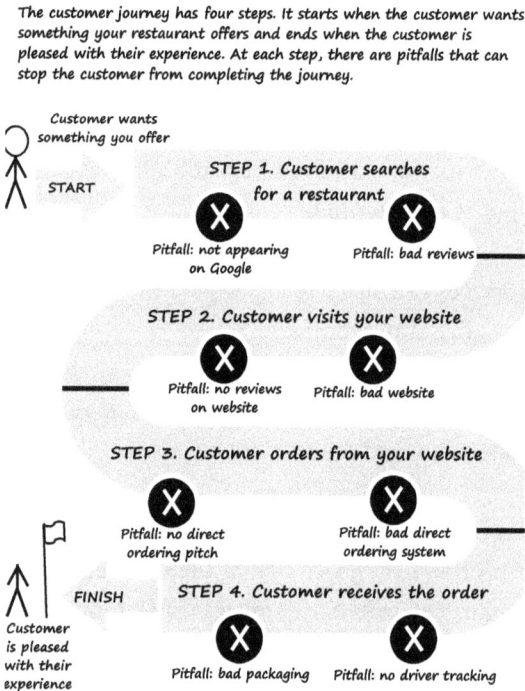

The customer journey has four steps. It starts when the customer wants something your restaurant offers and ends when the customer is pleased with their experience. At each step, there are pitfalls that can stop the customer from completing the journey.

Customer wants something you offer

START

STEP 1. Customer searches for a restaurant

Pitfall: not appearing on Google

Pitfall: bad reviews

STEP 2. Customer visits your website

Pitfall: no reviews on website

Pitfall: bad website

STEP 3. Customer orders from your website

Pitfall: no direct ordering pitch

Pitfall: bad direct ordering system

FINISH

Customer is pleased with their experience

STEP 4. Customer receives the order

Pitfall: bad packaging

Pitfall: no driver tracking

PITFALL 1: NOT SHOWING UP ON GOOGLE

The first point at which Bill's Pizzeria could have failed was when Megan searched online for a pizzeria in Santa Monica.

If Bill's Pizzeria hadn't shown up on Google, it would never have gotten the chance to feed Megan. She might have ordered from Domino's or a local competitor instead.

PITFALL 2: BAD REVIEWS

If Bill's Pizzeria showed up in the top three Google search results but didn't have the best reviews, Megan might not have ordered from it. Imagine that Bill's reviews averaged 3.8 stars, while the competitors' reviews averaged more than 4.0 stars. In that case, Megan would have had a 50 percent lower chance of choosing Bill's. If reviews of Wanda's Pizza Place averaged 4.4 stars, Megan would have been much more likely to order from Wanda's.

PITFALL 3: BAD WEBSITE

Another failure could have happened if the Bill's Pizzeria website didn't answer Megan's questions.

For example, imagine the website was just a huge picture of a pizza with no words, no reviews, and no menu preview. (This happens all the time, by the way.)

It might look pretty, but Megan would be confused by the website. It wouldn't help Megan answer her questions, so she would quickly click back to Google and into a competitor's website. Bill's website would have failed to understand the customer's experience.

PITFALL 4: NO REVIEWS ON THE WEBSITE

Imagine that Bill's website showed Megan the menu but didn't show her proof that people in her community like the restaurant. Seventy percent of people check online reviews before placing an online order, and there'd be no place on Bill's site for Megan to do that.

Megan might have clicked to another website, such as Yelp, to see reviews. But Yelp might have a partnership with a delivery app like Grubhub, so Yelp would encourage Megan to order via Grubhub.

If only there had been reviews on the website! Then Bill's Pizzeria could have had a new direct customer.

PITFALL 5: NOT COMMUNICATING WHY DIRECT ORDERING IS THE BEST OPTION

Another failure could have happened if Bill's Pizzeria didn't tell Megan why she should order from the restaurant's website rather than Grubhub. She might have ordered from Grubhub because she wouldn't have known the benefits of ordering directly (such as faster delivery and better prices).

PITFALL 6: BAD DIRECT ORDERING SYSTEM

Even if Bill's website convinces Megan that it's best to order directly, she'll only do so if it's easy and the website looks trustworthy.

She needs an easy-to-use ordering system. She doesn't want a hassle at checkout, like creating a new account and remembering a password.

Friction like that might have prevented her from ordering.

Friction also might have been created if the online ordering was on a different website that didn't have Bill's branding (like toasttab.com or chownow.com).

Megan would have hesitated, not knowing whether she should trust this new site. She might not know what the new website is and assume it's a competitor to DoorDash—and at that point, why not just order from DoorDash, where she already has an account? She might have stopped ordering and gone to DoorDash.

PITFALL 7: NO DRIVER TRACKING

If Megan doesn't get any status updates on where her food is, it creates a frustrating situation for both her and the restaurant. Megan and Rachel can't start their movie till the pizza arrives. But they have no idea when that might be.

Megan might call Bill's to ask for an estimated time. But it's likely that Bill's phone will be busy with other customer calls.

Megan calling
the restaurant

Restaurant
Owner

It doesn't help if the pizzeria website says that orders take an average of thirty minutes. Data shows that people get attached to those time estimates. So if the estimate was thirty minutes but delivery takes thirty-five minutes, Megan is likely to feel upset.

PITFALL 8: BAD PACKAGING

The last potential failure could have happened when Megan's order arrived at her apartment.

If the packaging didn't reinforce the brand of Bill's Pizzeria, it could have lowered Megan's perception of the order's value.

Many restaurants package their takeout orders using materials that don't match their dining-room experience.

For example, a high-end Italian restaurant may have beautiful heirloom plates and nice silverware in their dining room, but they package their takeout in a thin plastic bag that looks like it should hold dirty laundry, with no branding and flimsy plates. The careless packaging makes the customer feel like what they've ordered isn't made with care.

When done correctly, packaging is a superpower. It lets you reinforce your restaurant brand with customers even when they're not standing next to you.

Here's one example of great packaging that I've seen firsthand: my friend ordered something from True Food Kitchen on Door-Dash. When the order arrived, the packaging told him to order directly from the restaurant's website to save money next time! There was even a QR code for him to scan to order. When we opened the bag, we saw a flyer next to the food. It educated us in more detail about the benefits of ordering directly from True Food Kitchen's website or app.

The restaurant is using these tactics to take back the customers it has lost to third-party delivery apps. It's brilliant because flyers are cheap. Spending a few cents and taking a little extra effort to make a flyer is worthwhile to recover 30 percent in fees and the customer relationship.

When we look at the steps of the customer's journey, we see what you can do at each step to create a better guest experience and grow your business.

Here are seven key points:

1. Make sure your restaurant is one of the first results that Google shows people when they search for a restaurant like yours.
2. Design your website to answer customer questions in a logical order and to be easy to browse on any device.
3. Share reviews on your website that describe in detail what customers like about your restaurant.
4. Explain why it's better to order directly from your restaurant instead of using an outside delivery app like Grubhub.
5. Have an ordering system that makes ordering directly from you easy for the customer and is a better value than the alternatives. This means having your own app and a system that saves guests money when they use it to order from you.
6. Give guests delivery tracking and updates.
7. Package your takeout orders in a way that shows the care that goes into your food and represents your brand well.

The following chapters will describe each part of a system that helps take guests through the ideal journey, avoiding the pitfalls.

SECRET 2

Translate for Mr. Google

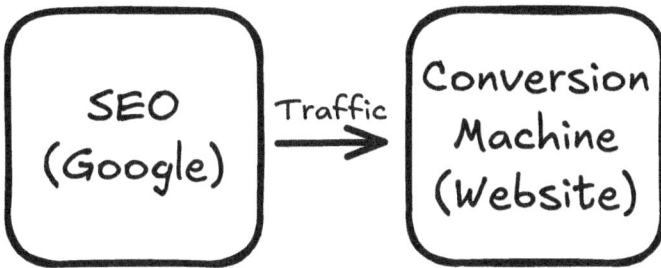

Being easy to find is important for a restaurant. But what makes restaurants easy to find today is different from what made them easy to find fifty years ago.

Fifty years ago, all you needed to do was have an attractive storefront in the middle of town and an ad in the Yellow Pages.

But today, being easy to find doesn't depend on those things. It depends on being visible online.

When some people hear this, they immediately think I'm talking about having a big social media presence. But that's not what I mean. As I mentioned earlier, the idea that you have to be active on social media is the number one lie that's killing restaurants.

Being easy to find online doesn't mean being on social media. It means being one of the first websites that come up when people do a Google search.

Remember Mo, from Talkin' Tacos?

His restaurant has more than 200,000 followers and thousands of likes on every post. With those numbers, you might expect social media to be the primary driver of Mo's growth.

But it's not.

When we track where Mo's customers are coming from, the data shows that social media accounts for less than 10 percent of his new customers.

Google, on the other hand, accounts for more than 90 percent.

Mo found that ranking high on Google searches was far more useful for growing his business than social media.

The lesson is clear: if you want to be easy for your customers to find, your restaurant has to be one of the first websites that come up when people do a Google search.

MEET MR. GOOGLE

To get recommended by Mr. Google, we first have to get to know what he looks for and how he sees the world.

Mr. Google

The easiest way for me to explain how Google works is to pretend that it's a person: Mr. Google.

Imagine that you type "pizza in Santa Monica" into the Google search box.

Mr. Google asks himself, "What are the best websites to show someone who's looking for Pizza in Santa Monica?"

Mr. Google decides which websites are best by looking for specific things on those websites. Based on what he finds, Mr. Google puts together a list of websites, ranked best to worst. Then he shows you the list.

Mr. Google evaluating your website

Mr. Google's checklist

Web page load speed ☑
Alt-text for images ☑
Contents fit screen ☐
High conversion rate ☐
Pages visited ☐
Technical blah blah ☐
blah blah blah... ☐

Your
website

Mr. Google
checking boxes

When Mr. Google evaluates websites, he's not looking for the same things you and I might look for if we were going to recommend a nearby pizza place.

Mr. Google can't sample the food. He can't experience the service. He can't appreciate the decor.

He instead judges websites by watching how people interact with them.

When Mr. Google looks at your website, he watches things like:

- how much time people spend on the site
- which pages they visit
- whether those pages adapt their images or text to fit on people's phone screens
- signs guests are getting what they want, like how many people end up converting into customers on the website

Your website must appear near the top of the list that Mr. Google gives people who are searching for restaurants like yours. That means your website has to speak Mr. Google's language. It has to have all the features that Mr. Google uses to evaluate websites.

Doing things so Mr. Google puts your website near the top of the list is called "search engine optimization." It's "SEO" for short. SEO is about telling Mr. Google why your restaurant is the best result. It's about ensuring that when people look online for something you provide, your business is the first they find. It's similar to what used to happen if you had a big ad in the Yellow Pages.

Mr. Google viewing images on your website

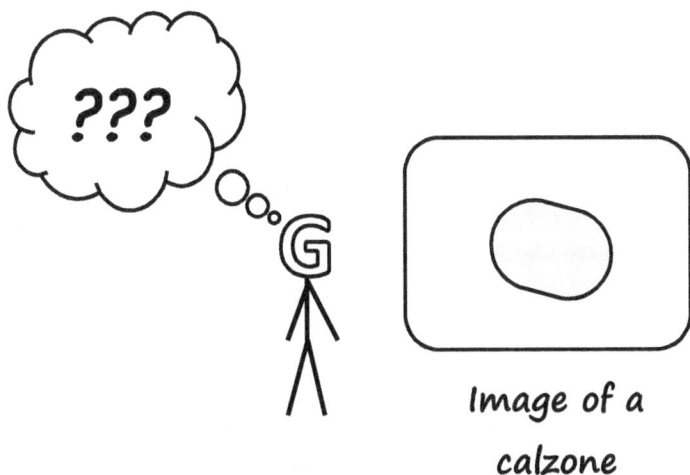

Image of a calzone

By the way, my team made a tool so you can see how Google "sees" your website. You get a score, and it tells you exactly what changes you need to make to improve. You can find it at grader. Owner.com.

Here's an example.

Imagine you want potential customers to know that your pizzeria offers calzones. You might think of putting a picture of a delicious calzone on your website.

The problem is that Mr. Google can't see images. So if all you do is put a picture of a calzone on your website, the message that you offer calzones is going to be completely lost on Mr. Google.

Instead, add some text along with the picture that says "picture of the best calzone in Santa Monica." Then Mr. Google will understand that your pizzeria offers calzones.

Knowing that you have to include text along with your pictures is part of knowing how to speak Mr. Google's language. It's part of ensuring that when people ask Mr. Google to look for something you provide, your website will be near the top of his list.

Mr. Google is also looking at how quickly your website loads. He doesn't want his users to have to wait to access a website that he's recommended. So he recommends faster websites over slower ones.

There's interesting research that shows that for every second a website visitor has to wait for a site to load, their chance of becoming a customer goes down by more than 20 percent.

Mr. Google also looks at the restaurant's review profile. He judges what the star rating of the restaurant is. He counts how many total reviews the restaurant has. He checks out how often people post reviews.

These are all signs of how popular a restaurant is. Mr. Google reads them so he knows where to send people when they ask him for the best option. The more often he sends guests to the best option, the more likely people are to keep asking him for future recommendations—which is how he stays in business!

CONNECTING GOOGLE, YOUR MENU, AND YOUR CUSTOMERS

Juan owns a taqueria in Orange County, California. When he created his taqueria, he wanted it to feel like an authentic Mexican place. He drew inspiration from his immigration to the United States and his love for his mother's cooking.

He titled all the dishes on the menu in Spanish. For example, instead of "chicken tacos," he would call the dish "tacos de pollo."

However, his restaurant was in a high-end area of Orange County where people didn't natively speak Spanish.

They had no idea what the authentic Mexican items were.

Juan was using the Spanish names with no translation.

Mr. Google viewing
a menu written in Spanish

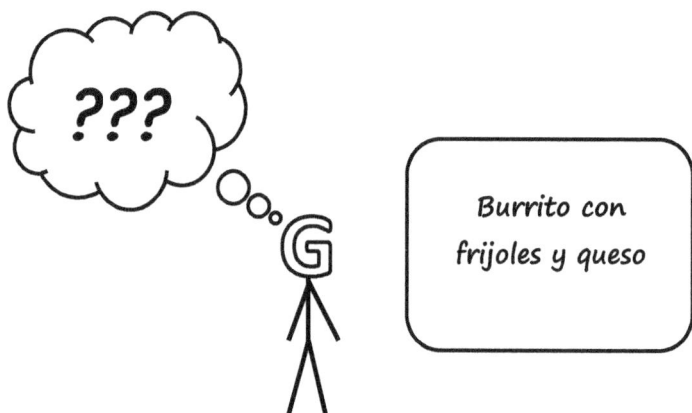

For his guests, it was a menu written in another language—one they didn't understand.

But something even worse was happening too.

When people googled "best chicken mole in Orange County" or similar, Juan's place wasn't showing up. Not because he didn't serve amazing chicken mole, but because *Google couldn't understand his menu.* When I met Juan, I showed him a tool called Google Keyword Planner. It lets you see (for free!) what people in your area are searching for and how many of them are searching for it every month.

For example, you can type in "chicken tacos in Orange County" and see that there are five hundred people a month searching for bean and cheese burritos in Orange County.

None of them are searching for "tacos de pollo," even though it might be the same dish. They know it as "chicken tacos."

That's how Juan realized there was a lot of demand in his area for his dishes, but people were searching for them using more generic English names. He was able to transform his menu to appeal to new customers and make his restaurant show up at the top of Google search results when people searched for these dishes in his city.

Juan's story is a case of trying to be too authentic and sticking too closely to a certain branding idea at the expense of menu-market fit. Today, Juan is still serving excellent food! And since his menu is easy to understand and searchable online, even more people can enjoy it.

This isn't just a Spanish thing or a non-English-language thing. I've seen similar issues when restaurants try to give their menu items fancy English names. But the common name, while it might seem generic, is really important for appealing to new customers.

For example, an Italian restaurant that sells garlic bread isn't going to help its business by calling the bread "Bread with a Special Something." (That's not a real example, but sometimes the real examples are just as bad.)

The point is that you need to use the words that customers would use to describe your dishes. You have to speak the language your customers are speaking. Otherwise, they won't have any idea what you're talking about.

That doesn't mean you can't get creative. For example, you can use some Spanish language in the food description, possibly in a sidenote to make it feel authentic. But don't write the entire menu in Spanish or complex English.

There's another cool way to use Google Keyword Planner. You can use it to decide what to offer on your menu! For example, imagine you have an Italian restaurant. Google Keyword Planner will tell you that there are always people searching for chicken parmesan in your area. It will even tell you how many people are searching for it every month.

For free.

This is powerful because if people are searching Google for the names of dishes, that means they don't have a go-to place for what they're craving.

Now that you know this, you can add chicken parmesan to the menu and become their go-to place for the dish.

Then you can follow the website advice we discuss in Secret 3: Build a Conversion Machine and make a page dedicated to chicken parmesan. You'll get exposure to the dozens of customers per month in your area looking for it. Nobody else in your area is doing this. For real. You have the opportunity to become the go-to place for a specific dish. It's there for the taking.

The specific "boxes to check" for Google tend to change often. The changes are fast-paced enough that it doesn't make sense to print them in a book.

But I keep an up-to-date list of specific things that you can do to rank at the top of Google search results. You can see it and get a free guide that shares all the details you need here:

Owner.com/secret-seo

Build a Conversion Machine

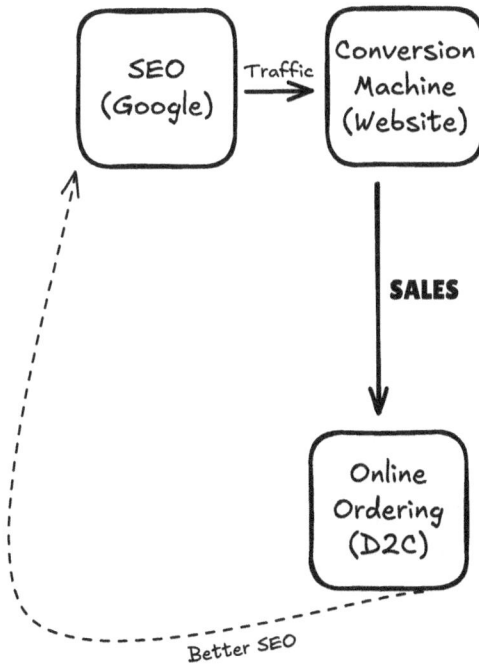

When I met Yuliana Vasquez in May of 2020, she was terrified. Overnight her restaurant, Somos Oaxaca, had flipped from getting dine-in traffic to relying on online ordering because of the COVID-19 lockdowns.

Yuliana thought she was prepared. She had an online ordering system on her website, and she believed her existing customers would order from her website to help her survive the pandemic.

The opposite happened.

Even though Yuliana had an online ordering link on her Wix website, nobody was using it. Her customers were ordering from her on the delivery apps.

That took her from having a profitable business in February to losing thousands of dollars per month by May.

Eventually, she was staring down two more months of survival.

Yuliana knew she needed a sustainable solution. All her sales were coming through Grubhub. She started researching and consulting with her restaurateur friends.

They pointed her to new technology for building a website and an online ordering system that people would prefer over Grubhub.

Doubtful at first, she wondered how people could prefer one website over another when both allowed ordering. Could she compete with Grubhub?

With just two months of cash left, she decided to take a chance.

She prayed she wouldn't have to go back to working in other people's restaurants, as she had before starting her own.

This business was her legacy, something to pass on to her kids.

She decided to try the new technology called Owner.com. It promised to build a website that would increase conversion rates and lead to more direct online orders.

I was on the other side of this. I had built the technology after seeing it change my mom's life.

When Yuliana signed up, we got to work. We started by figuring out how to communicate her restaurant's uniqueness to encourage direct orders.

Her old website was converting less than 1 percent of visitors into customers. By understanding customers' psychology and their decision-making process, we improved her website's conversion rate to more than 10 percent in three months.

This seemingly small change, from 1 percent to 10 percent, increased the number of orders from her website from two a day to twenty. That's an increase of more than five hundred orders a month.

This change not only helped her survive the pandemic but also allowed her to open a second location.

Over the past three and a half years, everything has changed for Yuliana and her husband. They went from being in survival mode to expanding their empire regionally. Her website was responsible for this huge change—specifically the redesign and rewrite of her website.

You may be skeptical: Does a website really make a difference to a restaurant's sales? Isn't a website just supposed to look pretty for the guest?

I used to feel the same way. I was most focused on driving people to the website by making it appear at the top of a Google search, not on the site itself.

But now I've seen Yuliana's before-and-after story happen again and again.

For example, it also happened for my friend Antoinette, the owner of Ottavio's.

Unlike Yuliana, Antoinette didn't start her restaurant; it has been in her family for generations. It's always done pretty well, but it was based in an older community in Lakeside right by a retirement home. At one point, Antoinette was struggling to acquire fresh customers.

So Antoinette decided to revamp her online presence. She focused specifically on building a new website.

The numbers she saw as a result are bananas!

Antoinette went from making less than $1,000 per month through her website (via online ordering) to more than $25,000 per month.

That's an increase of $24,000 per month in highly profitable takeout sales. And in just one year, her overall takeout business tripled.

Previously, Antoinette's website had been costing her sales by giving her guests a bad first impression. Now it's a superpower that's driving tons of sales.

Now that you see the power an amazing restaurant website can have, let's talk about what a website needs to grow sales.

In general, you need a website that does two things:

1. Convinces visitors to order your food (or to give you their email address if they're not yet ready to order from you)
2. Enables them to place their order directly with you instead of through an outside delivery app

I'll talk about the first point in this chapter. The second point is covered in the next chapter (Secret 4: Go D2C).

Let's start with what it takes to build a website that convinces visitors to order your food—or to give you their email address if they're not yet ready to order from you.

Here are ten things your website must have to convert visitors into customers:

1. Unique pages for each of your most popular items
2. A strong, clear hook at the top of the page (so the visitor doesn't have to scroll)
3. A tempting offer that invites people to share their name, email, and phone number

4. Social proof
5. High-quality images and alt text on every major menu item
6. A section that educates guests on ordering directly from the restaurant
7. Your restaurant's story
8. The jobs page
9. Brand consistency
10. A clear tracking system

I'm going to discuss each of these must-have items in detail.

As I go over each, I'll share real examples from real restaurants, including their website traffic and sales data.

I'll explain what they've done that has had a measurable impact on their revenue. I'll give you tips that you can act on regardless of what website builder you have—whether it's Wix, Squarespace, or some web guy running your website.

The tips are simple, so you don't have to be a tech geek like me to set them up. But you do need to understand them so you can hold the people who build your website (or the platform that powers your website) accountable for driving real sales growth for your business.

MUST-HAVE 1: UNIQUE PAGES FOR EACH OF YOUR MOST POPULAR COMMON ITEMS

Having a unique page for your food items probably sounds ridiculous. Does each dish really need its own page on the website? Yes—at least your most popular dishes do. They each need their own page, and ideally, all of your dishes will have their own pages over time.

Let me explain.

For every popular dish, like BBQ pork ribs or chicken tikka masala, there are dozens of people craving that dish in every city in the United States—craving it and searching for it on Google.

For example, let's say I want great angel hair pasta and I'm in Lakeside, California. I'm likely to search on Google for "best angel hair pasta in Lakeside, California." You'll notice that Ottavio's Italian Restaurant comes up twice in the top results for that phrase: once in the map result and once in the search results.

This is because it's the only Italian restaurant in the area that has a dedicated page for angel hair pasta in Lakeside, California. The page has a description of the dish, relevant reviews of the dish, and (of course) pictures.

Ottavio's gets forty-five new customers every month from Google, like clockwork. The reason is that they have pages for each of their most popular menu items. These pages appear in search results when people in the area search for the menu items online.

Ottavio's is the only restaurant in town that does that. They have no competition for these searches, and it's driving a ton of growth.

The best part is that getting those customers is free. All Ottavio's had to do was set up the pages once. No need to pay Google for every click. People come in like clockwork every month, without any cost.

Let's look at the math behind this strategy.

Even if five people per month in your area are craving and searching for each of your five most popular dishes—maybe those are pasta, garlic bread, cheese pizza, chicken parm, and calzones—that's twenty-five people every month.

If you can rank at the top of Google search results, that's twenty-five people who are almost guaranteed to click on your website. There they'll see delicious food pictures and good reviews.

And since they're already craving the dish they searched for, you can link them to your online ordering or reservation system directly on that page so they can get it from your restaurant right away.

By the way, ranking at the top of Google search results is easier than you think. We discussed this a bit in the last chapter when I described how you can use Google Keyword Planner to offer the dishes people are craving. From there, the trick is to create unique pages for your food items. You can use any website builder to do so: Wix, Squarespace, Owner.com. Of course, I'm biased toward Owner.com because I'm the CEO of the company. Owner makes creating unique food pages easier: its website builder has a feature that automatically creates a page with AI-written content for every key dish on a restaurant's menu. But this isn't an Owner.com commercial, so let's get into the restaurant website Must-Have 2.

MUST-HAVE 2: A STRONG, CLEAR HOOK AT THE TOP OF THE PAGE (SO THE VISITOR DOESN'T HAVE TO SCROLL)

It's no secret that attention spans are decreasing with the rise of social media. Studies by Nielsen Norman Group, a research and consulting firm on the website user experience, show that when somebody lands on a website, the home page has just seven seconds to grab their attention before they click away.

That's why we call it a hook.

According to that Nielsen research, 80 percent of the time people spend looking at a website occurs before they scroll.

Three Parts of an Ideal Homepage

Visitors can see the following items without having to scroll:

1. A <u>hook</u> that explains why you're different and better,
2. Beautiful <u>pictures</u> of popular dishes,
3. <u>Social proof</u>: great reviews showing how popular your restaurant is.

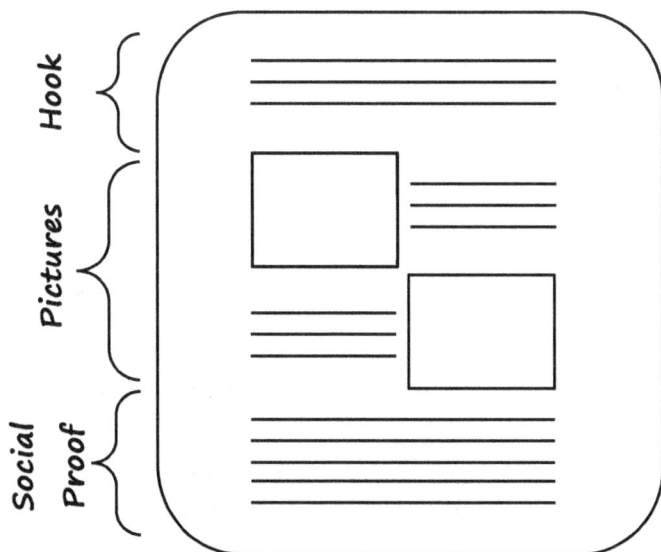

The average website visitor doesn't scroll at all before deciding to browse the website or go back to Google.

The precise term for "what you see before scrolling" is "above the fold."

Too many restaurant websites have a huge picture of food above the fold on their home page, and that's it.

While that food may look beautiful and delicious, it's not enough to keep somebody's attention today.

You need a hook to grab people's attention—without them needing to scroll.

The hook tells people why you're different and better than competitors. It needs to happen super quickly—it has to be the first thing they see.

What I've seen work best for the top of a restaurant's website is this combination of three elements:

1. A phrase that shares the restaurant's unique identity and, ideally, hints at their story (More on that later.)
2. A beautiful picture of the most popular dishes
3. Social proof, such as great reviews showing people how popular the restaurant is in its community or a number displaying how many orders have been placed today

With those three elements, you hook your website visitor enough to encourage them to scroll through the website.

But no matter how good a restaurant's website is, most visitors to the website won't convert into online orders or reservations—not right away.

That is why Must-Have 3 is so important.

MUST-HAVE 3: A TEMPTING OFFER THAT INVITES PEOPLE TO SHARE THEIR NAME, EMAIL, AND PHONE NUMBER

I know that might sound like gibberish. Let me explain.

According to a few studies I've seen, the average restaurant website converts about 1.5 percent of website visitors into paying customers. For the very best restaurant websites I've ever seen, that number is about 20 percent.

This means that even in the best case, 80 percent of people who visit your website aren't placing an order today.

So what can you do to earn money from the 80 percent? Can people who don't order the first time they visit your website be converted into customers later?

Yes, they can. You can collect their information and stay in touch with them. That's another important part of restaurant growth today. We will talk about this in more detail when we get to Secret 6: Defend Mindshare. But we'll preview it quickly right now.

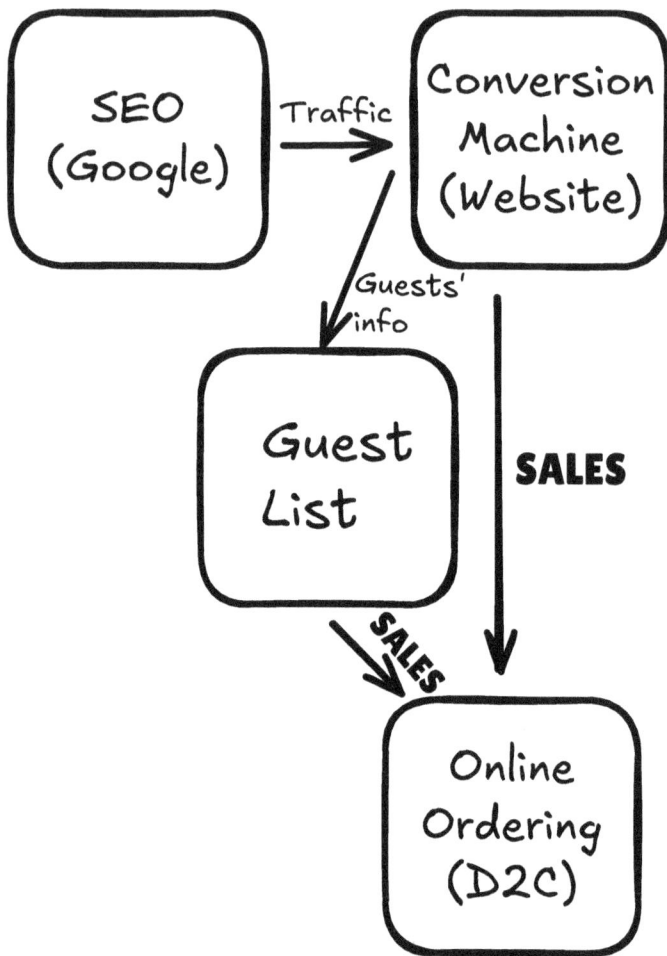

To get the most possible sales from a restaurant website, you need to convince as many visitors as possible to give you their name, email, and permission to market to them. (That permission is called a "marketing opt-in.")

All of the top-performing restaurant corporations—from Chick-fil-A to Texas Roadhouse and Sweetgreen—do this on their websites.

First, you need an obvious place where website visitors can give you their contact details and permission to market to them. Second, and more importantly, you need an offer that makes them want to share their information and receive marketing messages from you.

Here's what works really well for my friend Mo, the owner of Talkin' Tacos: he has a banner across the top of his website pages that says "Join our VIP club to get notified about discounts, specials, and events."

People can click on the banner and share their name, email, phone number, and birthday to join.

Then Mo uses that information for amazing automatic marketing, including emails and text messages to those people. He also uses the information to retarget those people on Facebook. (Retargeting means showing ads to people who have already visited your website.)

Finally, you need to make sure people trust you enough to give you their personal information. And there is one powerful way to convince people to trust your website: you have to show them that other people trust you.

I call that social proof.

MUST-HAVE 4: SOCIAL PROOF

Seventy-seven percent of guests check online reviews before choosing a restaurant.

Seventy-seven percent!

So how do you make this guest behavior work for you rather than against you? You add reviews to your website.

As I mentioned, the best-performing home page structure starts with a clear and compelling hook that visitors can see without needing to scroll.

Below that, you show beautiful pictures of your most popular menu items.

Directly after that, you have a section featuring your most awesome reviews.

When creating this review section, I like to step into the shoes of a guest looking for a new restaurant.

First, I need to look at the website to get a sense of what type of restaurant it is.

Next, I need to figure out what items they have that I might like.

Last, I need to see what other people are saying about the food. I need to make sure that the food is good and that I'm not missing any details before I order. The reviews, or social proof, will give me the information I need.

But the social proof shouldn't end on the home page. You can take it a step further. You can embed reviews on other pages too, like your online menu.

I saw my friend Rahul from Saffron Indian Kitchen do this very well on his website, SaffronOfPhilly.com. When you click on his most popular dishes, you see some reviews of those dishes right on the menu.

Soon after Rahul added reviews to his website, he saw a 25 percent increase in the rate of people placing online orders.

And since implementing all ten of the must-haves in this chapter, he's been making $50,000 more per month from direct online orders.

Part of the reason why sharing social proof on your website works so well is because it prevents people from going to review sites like Yelp for social proof. We all know how unfair those can be.

Unfortunately, review sites often have partnerships with Grubhub and other third parties. They try to get the guest to order from the delivery apps, which means the restaurant owner loses the profit and the customer data on the order. (We're going to talk about this much more in Secret 4: Go D2C.)

So it's best to provide the guest with a great website experience yourself. That way, people don't feel the need to go to third-party websites for reviews.

MUST-HAVE 5: HIGH-QUALITY IMAGES AND ALT TEXT ON EVERY MAJOR MENU ITEM

We all know menu pictures are important. But just how important are they?

Well, according to a report by Grubhub, high-quality pictures of a menu item can increase sales of that item by more than 30 percent.

So your website should have high-quality images of every major menu item.

But it turns out there's another way to use menu pictures on your website.

It's called alt text. It is invisible text that sits on each image and tells Google what the image is.

You might be wondering, "What's the point of that?"

The point is that if you set the alt text correctly, you can make your menu pictures show up first on Google Images.

Restaurant owners know that people love to eat with their eyes first. But they may not know that many people look for pictures of delicious food when they search online for restaurants.

Very few restaurants know that. So there's very little competition for the dozens of people every month in every city who are searching Google Images for menu pictures.

If you set up the alt text right, your pictures can take up several top spots in the search results.

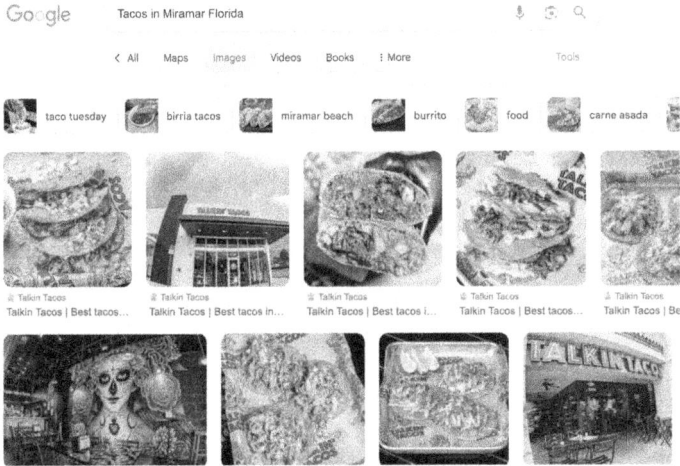

If we search for "Tacos in Miramar Florida," as thirteen hundred people per month do, six of the top nine image results are of Talkin' Tacos. My friend Mo owns that restaurant. He gets dozens of new customers at that location every month from Google Images.

They see his food in the top results, and it looks good. So they click on his website to learn more, see his reviews, and place an order.

Mo's pictures show up in the top results for Google Images because of alt text.

How do you use alt text?

In any website builder, when you're in edit mode, you click on an image and look for the alt text section that you type into.

Then you type:

Best [Name of Dish] in [City State]

For example:

Best Birria Tacos in Miramar Florida.

Then you click "Save," and—boom!—Google can now read and understand your images.

Adding alt text on menu item images has another important benefit: Americans with Disabilities Act (ADA) compliance.

You may have heard that restaurants get sued for having websites that blind people can't use. It's related to the ADA.

It's sad that this happens. It's mostly a scam by shady lawyers, but it does happen.

To protect yourself and comply with the ADA, set alt text for all images of your menu items. Setting alt text allows a braille reader to read the image.

So, in addition to attracting new customers through Google Images, this tip helps protect you against potential shakedowns from lawyers.

Okay, so we've now covered five strategies for getting website visitors and converting them into customers. But now we have to make sure they order from the online ordering system on your website, whether it's Toast, ChowNow, Owner, or another platform.

That brings us to Must-Have 6.

MUST-HAVE 6: A SECTION THAT EDUCATES GUESTS ON ORDERING DIRECTLY FROM THE RESTAURANT

Let's face it: telling people to order directly from your website to support your restaurant works with some guests, but not most.

Most people prefer the convenience of using the Grubhub app they already have on their phone. Apps also often make deals with credit card companies that give people bonus points when they use the app. They also offer free delivery through subscriptions like DashPass or Grubhub+.

Going in, your guests think it's more convenient and a better value to order from Grubhub and other third-party apps.

So how do you get those guests to order from you instead?

It's simple. You set up an online ordering experience on your website that is more convenient and a better value than the ordering experience on apps like Grubhub. And—this is important!—you educate them on why that's the case.

I call this an education section.

Ideally, you tell customers something like this:

Order directly from our website to get the best price and priority service, support local business, and earn free food via our rewards program.

That's it.

You just tell them the truth.

The truth is, you can save your customers money with the best price, and you can save them time with priority service. Even better, they can support local business and earn free food via loyalty points.

A lot of people are totally open to this! They just need to hear why it's good for them.

If you follow all of my advice in this book except for this must-have, you might see an increase in online orders. But the orders will still mostly come through the delivery apps. And we all know why that's a problem. It rhymes with losing all of our customer relationships—and all of our freakin' profit margin—to the enemy.

Okay, so the first six must-haves have been about getting new customers and increasing sales.

The next one is about increasing the number of people who want to support your business and order directly from you. It's also about increasing the love people have for your restaurant!

MUST-HAVE 7: YOUR RESTAURANT'S STORY

Your restaurant's story needs to appear in two places:

1. Your home page (this can feature a short version of the story)
2. A separate page dedicated to the restaurant's story

Why double down on your story?

Because people prefer to buy from individuals they know and trust, rather than faceless corporations.

This is the major advantage that local businesses have over big corporations.

The more your guests see your story and how your restaurant started, the more they will connect to you and care about supporting you.

You may be thinking, "My story isn't very interesting or fun."

But to guests ordering from you, it is!

People are curious about the people behind the businesses in the community they love.

Any restaurant's founding story can be interesting if you tell it the right way.

My story isn't that special.

But I want to know more.

Restaurant Owner   Guest

If you came here from Italy with nothing and saved up for seven years to pursue your dream of opening this restaurant, tell that story. Sharing it is powerful.

A lot of people are immigrants or come from immigrant families. They'll relate to that part of your story. Also, many people want to be entrepreneurs, and they will want to support you in pursuing your dreams.

If your restaurant is a family business with generations of ramen makers, tell that story.

If you fell in love with healthy eating on your trip to Los Angeles and wanted to create a place that gave people access to the same food in the Midwest, tell that story.

On the home page, create a section with a few sentences about your story. Link to a separate page where guests can learn more about you and your story.

Videos are ideal for storytelling because they make connecting to you easier, but text and pictures work great too.

We continually find that restaurants that tell their story have more repeat guests, higher average check sizes, and higher conversion rates. (The conversion rate is the number of website visits that turn, or "convert," into online orders.)

This section won't just attract guests; it will attract talent too. Potential employees want to know how the owner came to own their business. They want to know about the person they would be working for.

MUST-HAVE 8: THE JOBS PAGE

If you follow the other tips in this book, you're going to have many thousands of people in your community visiting your website every year. Maybe 1 percent of them are open to a role at a restaurant or know somebody who might be. Even if just 1 percent of website visitors are interested in a job, it can pay to have a place where they can submit a résumé online and learn more about the benefits.

Talkin' Tacos does this well with their jobs page. It simply says, "Join a growing team with good vibes and a love for good food."

Then it lists the benefits of working there: "Free Tacos. Growth Opportunities. Kind Coworkers."

Having this page gets them twenty-plus qualified applicants for positions every year. They don't have to pay Indeed or Craigslist. That's a huge bonus in this labor market!

Okay, so back to storytelling.

There's another important part of storytelling: brand consistency.

MUST-HAVE 9: BRAND CONSISTENCY

Pick any one of the top fifty restaurant brands in the United States. You'll see that their websites, their online ordering systems, their apps, and (of course) their dining rooms always have brand consistency.

The look, the feel, the language, and the story are the same everywhere. The logo is everywhere. The same colors are everywhere. Every part of interacting with them reinforces their story and who they are.

Why is this important? And why should you do this for your restaurant? Because it trains the guest to have a clear connection in their mind between your restaurant and a specific idea and feeling.

When guests see your colors or think of your type of food, you want them to instantly think of your restaurant.

If they have an unclear mental picture of who you are, they likely won't think of you next time they want to order takeout.

For example, think about Antoinette from Ottavio's. When guests nearby think of Italy or Italian food, we want them to visualize her classic Italian logo and colors and font and delicious pasta pictures. If her online presence is chaotic—if the website looks classic Italian, but the online ordering system looks generic and the Mailchimp emails look futuristic—what is the guest going to think of? Nothing at all. The brand is inconsistent and confusing.

Most people tend to be visual thinkers, and brand consistency plays into that fact. You can create brand consistency by giving guests clear visual connections to who you are.

I keep an up-to-date guide for restaurant branding. It includes step-by-step instructions on what to do for each aspect of your brand. You can see it if you visit:

Owner.com/secret-branding

MUST-HAVE 10: A CLEAR TRACKING SYSTEM

The biggest must-have for any website is performance tracking.

The tracking system will show you how effective your website is. It will tell you all kinds of numbers, including:

- how many sales your restaurant made thanks to your website

- how many new customers you got thanks to your website

If you don't know those numbers, how are you supposed to know if you should continue investing in your website? How are you supposed to know if your hard work is making a difference?

The most basic tracking system is Google Analytics.

It takes less than five minutes to install on any modern website builder, including Wix and Squarespace. It will instantly tell you how many people are visiting your website, where they are, and how many of them are clicking on each of your pages.

The problem I've found with Google Analytics, though, is that it doesn't integrate with any of the online ordering companies. It doesn't tell you how many sales you're getting because of your online marketing.

That's why my team and I built an analytics system, or tracking system, specifically for restaurants. Our customers can see which parts of their website are driving sales and new customers and which parts aren't—because we integrate analytics into the online ordering system of their website.

For example, the last time I looked at my friend Rahul's analytics dashboard for Saffron Indian Kitchen, he had gotten 345 new customers from online channels: 217 came from the website appearing in Google search results, 23 came from Facebook, 15 came from Instagram, and only 2 came from Yelp. It's a completely free service designed to give you a better understanding of how to make your restaurant succeed online.

Okay, so near the beginning of this chapter, I said that your website needs to do two things:

1. Convince visitors to order your food (or to give you their email address if they're not yet ready to order from you)
2. Enable them to place their order directly with you instead of through an outside delivery app

Secret 4 is all about that second point.

Let's talk about direct ordering and why it matters.

Go D2C

D2C stands for "Direct to Consumer." It's the term for companies selling their products directly to customers, without using any middlemen like stores or other businesses. Let's say a company makes sneakers. Normally, they might sell the sneakers through stores like Foot Locker, Target, and Zappos. As the customer, you'd go to one of those stores to buy the sneakers. But with D2C, the company sells the sneakers directly to you, through their own website or app.

For restaurants, "go D2C" means "sell food to your customers through your website, not through delivery apps."

Many restaurants have an ordering system on their website, but they still haven't gone D2C.

Most of their customers are still using delivery apps instead of ordering directly. And we all know this means the restaurants aren't making a profit on those orders. Even worse, they can't contact the customers afterward.

But there's yet another, secret problem. Google awards better rankings based on D2C sales. Google isn't paying attention to Grubhub orders. So if your customers are ordering on Grubhub, it's also hurting your SEO ranking.

Mr. Google wants to see D2C ordering. That's why "Online Ordering (D2C)" is connected to "SEO (Google)" in the Restaurant Growth System.

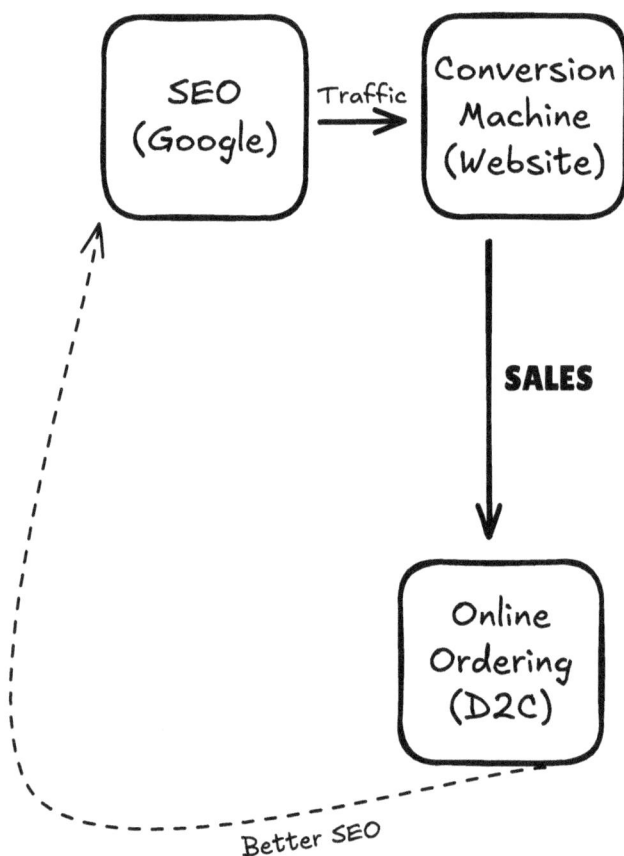

One of the most shocking experiences I've had in seven years of working in online marketing was related to D2C. It happened about three years ago. I was meeting a potential customer, Mike, for the first time in person.

Mike had found out from one of our sales reps that the CEO of Owner.com (me!) was in the area. He was considering buying our product for his restaurant down the street, so he reached out. He asked to come by the hotel where I was staying to talk to me. I agreed, excited to meet a potential customer. My team and I thought his pizzeria would be a great addition to our platform.

At one point after he arrived, I was telling him about Owner's online ordering system.

"It's going to help you drive more direct online orders," I said. "So you can avoid paying third-party fees."

He interrupted me. "Adam, I already have my own online ordering system."

He was adamant that he already had what we were offering. He didn't think he needed our solution. I tried to explain how our system was better, but he wasn't convinced. He repeated that he already had a system.

Then I said, "You've come all this way. I'd love to try some of your food. Did you bring any?"

He said no, so I suggested ordering from his restaurant.

To my surprise, he pulled out his phone to use DoorDash to order from his own restaurant!

At first I thought he wanted to show me how DoorDash compared to his direct online ordering system.

But then he placed an order through DoorDash.

Let me just put my order into DoorDash.
Why are your using DoorDash to order from your own restaurant?
Restaurant Owner
Adam

I asked him, "Mike, I thought you had your own ordering system. Why are we ordering from DoorDash?"

He replied, "Oh, it's so easy and convenient. Going to a website is too frustrating."

This was a lightbulb moment for me. If the restaurant owner preferred a third-party app for its convenience over his own website or app, how could he expect his customers to order directly?!

It led me to start asking on sales calls, "When you order your restaurant's food, where do you order from?"

More than 90 percent said they used delivery apps!

When I asked why, they said it was easier and that they got points for credit card rewards.

I realized it wasn't enough to create a better experience for the restaurant. We needed to create a better experience for the *guest*.

We needed to find a way to make the guest *prefer* to order directly from the restaurant.

That shifted our focus from optimizing the website just for the restaurant to optimizing it for the guest too. We had to also focus on creating a guest experience that makes people want to order directly.

Our goal was that restaurant owners would proudly use their own app or website and tell people about it rather than feeling embarrassed by it.

The guest is going to make their decision about how to order based on what's best for them. They don't care what's better for the restaurant—at least, 95 percent of people don't. That's what our numbers show.

But they definitely care about what's best for themselves.

Specifically, customers tend to care about three things for themselves:

1. **Ease:** a way of getting their food that's fast and easy
2. **Value:** a way of getting their food that costs less money
3. **Trust:** a way of getting their food that makes them feel confident and safe

EASE

One thing people really care about is ease (a.k.a. "convenience"). Ease has become the most important thing that people optimize for in their lives. They hate hassles. They hate waiting for long periods of time. They want everything now and in the easiest possible way.

Is it fast and easy?
Does it cost less?
Is it safe?

Guest thinking of how to place her order

Think about how you buy most of the things you need. For ordering household items, you probably use Amazon because they have a mobile app that you are signed into. It enables you to quickly add to your cart and check out, so you can get what you need in less than two minutes. Groceries are now delivered by Instacart and other delivery services. And restaurants, of course, are increasingly being taken over by Grubhub and other apps.

Delivery apps and typical restaurants' websites are like night and day. Ordering from delivery apps is way more convenient than ordering from a restaurant's website.

So the first question is, "How do we combat that difference and make it faster and more convenient to order directly from restaurants?"

We start by looking at the online ordering experience so we can learn how to improve it.

Guests face a few obstacles in the average online ordering experience.

First, it's inconvenient for guests to have to log in with a username and password every time they visit a website. Most people won't remember their password for that Italian restaurant they order from twice a month, so making them constantly sign in with a username and password significantly reduces ease.

It's even worse if the system doesn't support Apple Pay and Google Pay. People don't want to type in their credit card details manually.

Your online ordering experience has to be smooth if you want to succeed in going D2C.

To help you understand the perfect D2C guest experience, I'll share the one that I've spent the past seven years building at Owner. This is not an Owner commercial. I'm telling you about Owner's D2C guest experience so you can hear about real examples. There are other systems that have most of the features I will mention, but Owner offers them all in one place. At the end of the chapter, I will link to a list of multiple vendors that you can use to go D2C.

There are a couple of things your restaurant needs in order to have a smooth, convenient D2C guest experience.

Convenient payment is one of the most important pieces. Ideally, your online ordering system supports Apple Pay and Google Pay so guests don't need to type in their payment details. Some guests may want to save their details, so your online ordering system should also support that. On Owner.com, guests can create an account and save their details. Owner's system is based on phone numbers. Guests get a six-digit code to sign in each time, so they don't have to remember a password.

Another big driver of ease is time to delivery. People want their food as soon as possible. That's why restaurants should tell customers they'll give them faster service if they order directly through their system. Restaurants should put direct orders at the front of the line. They should make sure customers who order directly don't wait as long as customers who order through third-party apps. The message is "You're supporting us, so we'll support you."

The ultimate convenience for guests who order multiple times a month is an app on their smartphone's home screen that allows them to order quickly. The app elevates your restaurant to a higher status—right next to Instacart, Amazon, and Grubhub. With the app, ordering directly from you is just as easy as ordering from Amazon. There's no need to search for the website, click on it, or log in each time. Within thirty seconds, repeat customers tap on the app, to which they're already signed in, and see their go-to order front and center on the screen.

The mobile app enables a guest experience that is similar to the guest experiences at the biggest tech companies, from Uber to Instacart and Amazon. Everything is becoming on-demand, app-based, and mobile-first, yet the online ordering experience at most restaurants isn't. The big restaurant corporations, however, are mobile-friendly. At Domino's and Sweetgreen, for example, more than 50 percent of total orders go through their mobile app. This is a massive trend! Your regulars—your most important customers—will appreciate this convenience.

VALUE

Ease aside, there's another factor people optimize for: affordability and good value. Today Grubhub and other delivery apps tend to beat restaurants at this. They've been clever in setting up subscriptions like DashPass, which gives people free delivery, or credit card points as a bonus for each transaction.

How do restaurants offer guests better value than Grubhub does?

First, they have to create an experience that saves guests dollars. Grubhub takes 30 percent of the total transaction from the restaurant, but they also take an average of 20 percent from the guests with extra fees: delivery fee, convenience fee, and service fee. A guest's fifty-dollar transaction on Grubhub quickly becomes sixty dollars or more with all the fees the app tacks on. When people order directly from your restaurant, you don't need to hit them with 20 percent in fees. They can save dollars right away.

But—this is important—you can't be subtle about this! You have to tell customers they're saving eight dollars on their food by ordering from you instead of from third-party apps. The way we do this on the Owner system is similar to how Instacart constantly tells customers that they're saving X amount of hours every time they place an order. We tell guests throughout the ordering experience that they're saving X amount of money by ordering from the restaurant directly rather than through a third-party app. We educate them on why ordering directly is a better value.

But the better value doesn't end there. Restaurants can offer more value by building a gamified loyalty system into the ordering experience. This takes a page out of the playbook of the most successful restaurants.

Chick-fil-A, for example, has a loyalty system that has helped them build the most loyal customer base on planet Earth. Owner.com has modeled ours after theirs. For every dollar customers spend at a restaurant, they get points, and those points can unlock different food rewards.

You might think food rewards will drive up food costs and wipe out profit margins. But Chick-fil-A created a loyalty system that doesn't allow customers to unlock the entire menu. It allows customers to unlock free rewards only on menu items with very low food cost: appetizers, drinks, and desserts. The food cost of these items is always less than 10 percent.

For example, while a restaurant might sell cheese fries for seven dollars, the food cost for the cheese fries is thirty-five cents. The restaurant can give customers cheese fries with every order to thank them for being loyal. Customers feel like they're getting a seven-dollar value, but it costs the restaurant just thirty-five cents.

Or a restaurant can let customers earn points for ordering directly from them. When customers earn enough points, they can choose an appetizer, drink, or dessert with a seven-dollar value (but a low food cost).

This economic hack is the most powerful way to drive customer loyalty. It creates a perception of generosity. The customer thinks, "Woah, how are they so generous? They're giving me a seven-dollar value for free! I can get my own appetizer, beverage, or whatever I want." Meanwhile, to the restaurant, the food cost is just a tiny fraction of that value.

Another note on the online ordering experience: your online ordering system should know which menu items pair well with each other. It should suggest that the guest add complementary items to their order.

For example, maybe you know that when somebody orders a chicken parmesan dish, they're much more likely to order the molten lava cake for dessert or the garlic bread as an appetizer. Why not suggest these items during the online ordering process?

TRUST

A final point to keep in mind: you need to maintain trust with your customers. They don't want to leave your website and navigate to an outside app to place their order. That breaks the relationship of trust you built with them while they've been on your website. Having a direct ordering system creates a better experience for them. It also makes more money for you because you no longer have to depend on delivery apps!

I have seen hundreds of restaurants become independent from delivery apps by creating their own online ordering systems. You can do this too.

IT ISN'T JUST ABOUT THE FEES

Apps like Grubhub charge a lot, and that's why direct ordering is better for you. But the fees aren't the only reason to have your own ordering system. This is about having ownership of what you've built.

Your customer base is your most valuable asset. At every restaurant, the regular customers make sales and profits consistent.

But delivery apps take that away. When customers order from them, the apps own the customer relationship—not the restaurant.

That means that the restaurant has lost its most valuable asset. And when third-party apps own the customer relationship, they block the restaurant from communicating with its own customers.

The research shows that it's seven times cheaper to increase sales when you market to existing customers versus strangers: Telling guests about specials. Reminding them to reorder. Inviting them to try new menu items. None of that is possible when the delivery apps don't share guests' names anymore—not to mention their email address, phone number, or marketing opt-in preference.

As promised, you can find a link to a list of vendors that you can use to go D2C here:

Owner.com/secret-direct

Capp-Ture Your Regulars

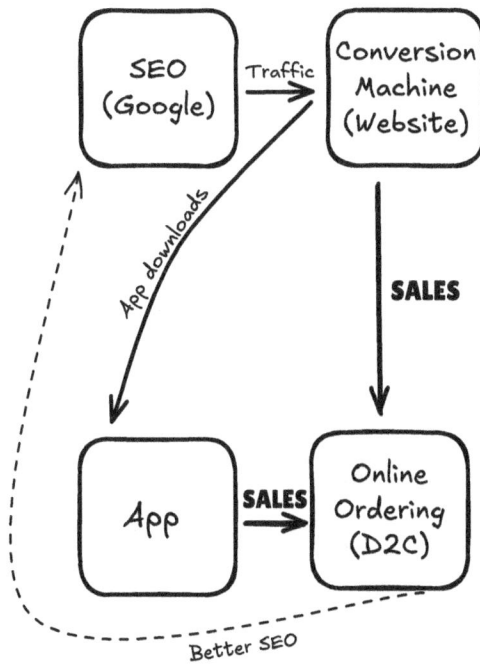

This secret seems like a bad idea. Even I was against it for many years. I have to thank Antoinette Belvedere, owner of Ottavio's Italian Restaurant, for making me see it. Hers was the first restaurant my team set up with its own app.

If you're a corporate chain, having an app is normal. Starbucks has an app. So do Sweetgreen, Cava, and most of the other major restaurant chains you can name.

For years, I assumed the reason people download those apps is that the app enables them to order across multiple locations.

I assumed a restaurant like Ottavio's, which has just one location, couldn't benefit from an app.

Even if it could, I assumed the app would cause more problems than it would solve.

Turns out I was 100 percent wrong.

Antoinette harassed me about this every day for a year.

She'd text me and call me about it. When we'd speak, she'd say, "Adam, I have the easiest time ordering my coffee from Starbucks. It's the simplest experience. All I do is open the Starbucks app. It's already got me signed in, gives me loyalty points, and within thirty seconds I can place my go-to order.

"But when people order from us, we're expecting them to go through all these difficult steps where they first have to find our website, then click into the website, find the 'Order Now' button, click that, and then log in every time because it's a website. After they log in, they go through a time-consuming process. We should have our own Ottavio's Italian Restaurant app."

I knew her customers at this point. Antoinette had been my customer for a while, so I knew she was located in a retirement community surrounded by people aged fifty-five to ninety.

I told Antoinette, "There's no way your customers would ever go for an app. If there's any restaurant an app wouldn't work for, it's yours. I appreciate the suggestion, but I don't think we're going to invest."

But she just kept asking. So, finally, I said, "Okay, fine. We're going to launch an app for you and also for another restaurant with totally different customers. We'll see whether there's actually demand for this."

So we built the app for Antoinette.

Within thirty days, more than 50 percent of Antoinette's total takeout volume was flowing through her app.

All of her "old people" had simply downloaded the app! She hadn't even bribed them with anything.

APPS AREN'T JUST FOR YOUNG PEOPLE

The big insight from that story is that the app isn't just for young customers. It also isn't just for large corporations. The app is the best experience for regulars who consistently order from restaurants again and again and again.

The reason is that the app makes the experience so much faster for those regulars. It's ten times faster. And it's frictionless: there's no need to sign in every time or find a website. Customers just tap on the restaurant's icon on their phone's home screen, and within thirty seconds, they can buy their regular order and earn loyalty points.

I've now rolled out custom apps across thousands of restaurants, and I've seen the successful numbers again and again.

The mobile app has become a game changer in their businesses. It enables them to provide an experience to the guest that is much more like ordering from national brands. That is, customers have an icon on their home screen to click, they're already signed in, and all their details are stored.

Before App

After App

It takes a few seconds to order on a mobile app. Customers no longer have to navigate to the website, which typically requires searching Google for the restaurant name and clicking "View Website." They also don't have to log in to the online ordering system. Having an app shortens the ordering process from minutes to seconds. This is why all fifty of the top restaurant corporations in the United States have their own apps.

HOW THE APP HELPS YOU MAKE MORE MONEY

We tracked Ottavio's customers, and we compared those who used the app with those who didn't. Over the course of six months, we found that customers who used the app spent over 50 percent more.

They ordered at a higher frequency and made larger transactions.

Because the app made it easier for ordering to become a habit, customers more quickly became regular customers (a.k.a. "whales").

We haven't even discussed push notifications yet. Push notifications are magical; they're like texting but less annoying.

Within seconds, you can send a message to all customers who have your app installed, reminding them to reorder their favorite dish. You can buzz their phone and tell them, "Hey, it's Friday night. We have your calzone waiting!" The notifications simplify the customer experience, making it much easier to reorder from you.

Another major benefit of the app is called "location services."

This is crazy. Apps let you ask customers to share their location. This means that you can see people's locations—and you can say hello to them when they pass by your location.

Domino's does this in an amazing way. If you have their app and you drive by one of their stores, your phone will say, "Hey, a Domino's is right down the street. We'd love to see you."

That is incredibly powerful. You can remind people to order food when they're nearby. Location services also make it much easier to expand to multiple locations. You can see the locations of your customers and use that in automated marketing, and you can use it to decide where to open another location. When expanding to franchising, you can use the data you collected from location services to describe your unique sales path. Cava had an app from the beginning, so they could tell their private equity investors, "We have our own app, we know where all our customers are, and we know so much about them. With your investment, we can expand to cities where we know we have a huge customer base."

A friend once asked me, "Is there any restaurant that should not have an app?"

Yes. Any restaurant that doesn't count convenience as a major part of their appeal.

For example, think of a fine-dining restaurant. Their whole experience is built around slowness. They serve eight-course meals that take hours to eat. It's the opposite of convenience. They also typically don't do takeout. Since the app is about convenience, it could backfire by contradicting a fine-dining restaurant's story.

An app is probably also a waste of time for an airport restaurant or a restaurant in a tourist destination like Disney World. In those cases, there aren't going to be many regular customers. The customers for those restaurants are all transitory. There aren't any regulars for the restaurants to capture with an app.

Those restaurants are the exceptions. For everyone else, an app is a good idea. It can be truly magical for regular customers who want the easiest way to repeatedly order from a restaurant.

The best part is that customers do not have to be convinced to use your app.

Think about everything that people frequently buy, such as household goods on Amazon or groceries on Instacart. So much shopping today happens on apps—it's a major way these businesses function.

So when you tell customers that they can use an app to simplify something they do multiple times a month (ordering from you), it's obvious to them that it will save them time.

All you have to do is remind them of all the time they will save. You can do this with a small section on your website that says "Order faster using our app."

That's all you need, in most cases, to get most of your customers to use your app instead of calling you and jamming up your phone line or ordering from Grubhub.

Defend Mindshare

Restaurant Growth System

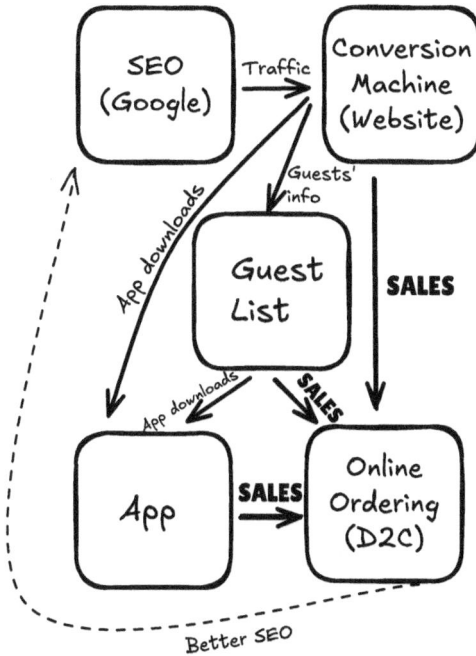

Within the four walls of the dining room, restaurant owners have this concept of "table touches." You go up to tables of people who are eating your food, and you introduce yourself.

You say, "Hey, I'm the owner. My name is Phil. It's great to meet you. How are you liking your food?"

The guest feels extra valued because the owner is reaching out to them and developing a relationship.

But when orders are placed digitally, you don't have that same opportunity to touch their table. The dining room is now in the customer's living room.

You can't physically go to every customer's house to ask, "Hey, how's your food?"

But you can use your guests' emails.

Emailing your guests is like scaling that table touch. You're still following up after customers get the food. But you're doing it with many people at the same time, no matter where you personally are and no matter where your food is being enjoyed.

At Owner.com, we set this up for our customers. After an order, their system automatically sends a feedback email asking, "Hey, how was your food?"

Customers can click on it and tell the restaurant how their food was.

This is helpful whether they loved the food or not.

If the customer had a positive experience, the restaurant owner can say, "Oh, I'm so glad it was a positive experience. Thanks for letting me know. So glad you loved our lasagna." That makes the customer feel valued.

But if they had a negative experience, this is your chance to make it right before it ends up on Yelp. According to the data I've seen, a typical negative review costs a restaurant $700 in new sales from new customers. You can prevent that from happening if you stay in touch with customers and respond to feedback.

PEOPLE DON'T SUDDENLY HATE YOUR FOOD

We've all had this experience as guests of other people's restaurants. We love a restaurant; they serve our favorite food. We order from them at least once a week. We go there in person and enjoy the dining room too.

Then one day we leave that restaurant, and life happens.

Something interrupts our pattern. Maybe we go out of town or some event causes us to break our habit of going to the restaurant.

The restaurant didn't do anything wrong. We don't suddenly hate their food. Still, over the next few weeks, we just forget about that restaurant. The restaurant doesn't remind us to come back or order, so we don't remember to go back.

Then months, even years, pass, and eventually, we remember, "Oh my gosh, Bill's Pizzeria was the best. What happened to that place? We should order from them again."

And we do.

But in that period, Bill's Pizzeria lost out on all that potential business. In some cases, customers might never return.

In this very noisy world, restaurants get forgotten. It's not because people suddenly start to hate their food. It's because there's just so much noise.

Unless restaurants are loud enough in their messaging and consistent enough in how frequently they communicate, people forget or lose track of them.

The solution to this problem is ensuring that once a customer has either dined at your restaurant physically or ordered digitally, you don't lose touch with them. You send them messages reminding them of what they loved about the experience, and you tell them more about your story, upcoming events, or specials to keep them engaged.

The official term for this is "marketing automation."

Marketing automation enables restaurants to stay top of mind with thousands of people. It allows them to send emails and text messages to guests based on their past ordering behavior. This gets them to not only continue ordering but also think more and more highly of the restaurant's brand.

A lot of restaurant owners are hesitant about this idea. So I want to talk point-blank about the fear of marketing.

FACING THE FEAR OF MARKETING

Have you ever had a neighbor from hell? I have.

It was after I moved to the San Francisco Bay Area—the technology capital of the world. Living there has its perks, but it also led to an outrageous disaster with my neighbor. Let's call him Ron.

It all started about a year after I moved into my building. Ron came up to me one day as I was getting into the elevator and started asking questions.

"Hey, man. How did you raise money?"

I was a bit taken aback because I had never met Ron before, so I didn't know how he even knew I had raised money.

That day, I politely answered his questions.

The very next day, Ron was at it again. He saw me leaving the building and beelined to me. Within two minutes, he was asking me for introductions to my investors.

I'm a non-confrontational person by nature, so I didn't want to upset Ron, but he was making me feel uncomfortable. I asked him, "How did you know about my startup before we had met?"

He told me that he saw my name on my mail, typed it into Google, and realized that I was the co-founder and CEO of Owner.com.

My jaw dropped at that moment. I politely replied, "Wow, okay!"

and said I wasn't ready to make investor introductions at this point.

Little did I know that he would take that to mean that he should talk to me every day as I was leaving my apartment, in case I'd changed my mind. So that's what he did.

For three straight months, anytime I saw him in the hallway, he would ask me for investor introductions. Again and again and again.

After months of this, I ended up taking care of Ron. (No, he's not in my freezer. But I basically convinced him that he'd have more luck in a different city.)

When it comes to marketing, many restaurant owners have a deathly fear of being like Ron. And it's a reasonable concern. A lot of the restaurant marketing out there just repeatedly asks for the same thing. It feels like harassment to guests. After that first reminder to order your tacos, or the second, or the third—it gets old. It can even seem aggressive, or like you're trying too hard to get customers to buy.

DON'T BE LIKE RON

If Ron had gotten to know me, shared more about his story, and built a relationship with me over time, I would have been happy to help him. We might've even become friends.

Like Ron, you have control over the message you send to people. You can choose to send messages that are relevant and personalized to your customers.

For example, a good marketing email feels like a personalized note from a friend. It finds people at the right time, and it contains relevant and valuable information.

If you constantly tell your customer to buy the same dish from your restaurant, that's not relevant or valuable. But when you vary the message, it becomes novel, relevant, and valuable. Some emails can tell customers about dishes they might like based on what they enjoyed in the past; other emails can tell them about upcoming events or the founding story of the restaurant.

So, no, repeating the same "buy, buy, buy" messaging doesn't work. But keeping in touch with customers does.

Almost every business with more than $1 million in revenue has adopted the practice of regularly emailing customers.

This means that if you don't stay in touch with your customers, your competitors will.

Why lose that advantage to your competitors out of fear of being too pushy, when you can simply avoid being pushy?

Let's discuss what works when emailing customers. We'll talk about marketing that's helpful but not pushy.

THE FOUR TYPES OF EMAIL MARKETING CAMPAIGNS FOR RESTAURANTS

As I mentioned earlier, there are really only three ways to grow your restaurant: get more customers, turn them into repeat customers, and increase the size of each order.

In email marketing, we always focus on those three paths to growth.

There are four types of automated campaigns that restaurants can set up. A campaign is a series of pre-written emails that you send to customers using email marketing software. These campaigns ensure that your customer always moves forward through the journey from just visiting your site to being a loyal fan.

CAMPAIGN 1: VISITOR → CUSTOMER

At the very beginning of the customer journey, a potential customer visits your website. But, for whatever reason, they're not yet ready to order. They're not a customer yet. They're just a visitor.

In fact, that's what happens most of the time. We know from earlier chapters that at least 80 percent of people won't order on their first visit to your website.

If your website is set up properly, you can offer them something in exchange for their email address.

For example, you could have a banner on your website that promises something like "Opt in to future deals, hear about new menu items, and join our VIP club online."

If the website visitor likes the promise, they will share their email address and name. Let's imagine this visitor's name is Ellen. (I'm calling her a visitor because she's not a customer—yet.)

After collecting Ellen's email, you can send her a series of automatic messages that gradually take her from being interested in what you offer to becoming a new customer.

4 Types of Marketing Campaigns

Campaign 1

Visitor ➔ Customer

Campaign 2

Customer ➔ Repeat Customer

Campaign 3

Regular Revival

Campaign 4

Repeat Customer ➔ Whale

It's important that immediately after receiving Ellen's email address, you send her an email.

Some restaurants make the mistake of waiting too long to send an email. A common trap is manually sending emails to every customer once every week or two. The problem is that if you wait a week after Ellen has shared her email address with you, she'll likely forget that she opted in to your restaurant's emails. Your email will almost look like spam.

The best practice is to send an email right away, automatically. The first email needs to give Ellen a clear and compelling reason to order from the restaurant.

What usually works best is a one-time discount with a time limit—especially if you highlight one or two of the most popular dishes. For example, you might send Ellen an email offering a free lava cake with her first order, this week only.

Most customers won't convert on that first email. That's okay! You can send them another email. But this one should not bug them to place an order.

Instead, use this second email to start gradually building a relationship with Ellen.

One effective option is to send an email that comes from you, the owner. In that email, introduce yourself and tell Ellen why you started the restaurant. You could also tell the story behind the most popular dishes. This will help Ellen feel a deeper connection to your restaurant.

Then, a couple of days later, you can send another email telling Ellen about an upcoming event, like Fun Friday (maybe people can come and play cornhole in your dining room). This email gives Ellen another glimpse of your restaurant.

The point of this email campaign is to stay in touch with people who haven't made an order until they do so. You want to change the angle and approach of every email so that over time, you're developing more trust with the people who receive them. Eventually, Ellen will place an order. Congrats! You've succeeded in the visitor-to-customer campaign.

CAMPAIGN 2: CUSTOMER → REPEAT CUSTOMER

Now you have an awesome new customer. The next campaign is about turning this brand-new customer, who's ordered from you once, into a regular customer who orders from you repeatedly.

For this campaign, you can use tactics similar to those you used for the visitor-to-customer campaign. I don't recommend starting with an offer, though, because the customer has already ordered.

Instead, you can tell the customer about other menu items they might like based on what they ordered—for example, "Hey, Ellen, if you liked our calzones, you're gonna love our Chicago-style pizza. It also has our signature house-made dough and delicious mozzarella cheese, but it's easier to share! Try it out." You're cross-selling the menu, so Ellen starts to crave more items from your restaurant.

If that doesn't resonate with Ellen, or even if it does, the next email could be the story of how the pizzeria came to be, followed by an update about another upcoming event.

The messaging is similar to what you would use to make website visitors become customers—but you don't lead with a discount. Instead, you try to grow the customer's desire for your food by sharing other menu items they might like.

Here's an example of a tactic that works surprisingly well. A week after Ellen places her first order, but a couple of hours earlier in the day, you can email or text her a reminder of your food.

You can say something like "Hey, it's Friday night again. Feeling like that calzone? Click here to order it in one tap." This helps Ellen start to build a behavior around ordering a calzone on Friday nights.

I learned this from the head of analytics at Domino's. They are masters of reinforcing the customer's order at the same time each week. People tend to have the same routines on the same days of the week, so sending them a well-timed invitation to order can create a habit.

This idea ties into the Hooked model created by Stanford researcher Nir Eyal. He describes the Hooked model in a fascinating 2014 book called *Hooked: How to Build Habit-Forming Products*. In particular, the book explains how people get "hooked" on apps like Instagram. But you can also get people "hooked" on your restaurant. The model is surprisingly relevant to restaurants. It can help you build ordering behaviors. That's what I'm going to focus on here.

The Hooked model has four parts: Trigger, Action, Investment, and Variable Reward. I'll first explain the model using the example of a social media app.

Part 1. Trigger: Something That Initially Connects the Customer with the Product

With a social media app, the first trigger might be your friend telling you to get on the app. Once you've downloaded the app, the trigger might be a notification reminding you to check what's happening on the app.

Part 2. Action: A Simple Step That Users Can Take to Get What They Want

In the social media example, the action could be downloading or opening the app.

Part 3. Variable Reward: A Reward That's Fulfilling Yet Leaves the User Wanting More

Whenever you do anything on the app, the app rewards you in slightly different ways. You get some likes and some comments. The more you scroll, the more content you see. The reward is a little different each time, but you can always expect some reward for using the app.

Part 4. Investment: A "Bit of Work" That the User Does to Get Their Reward, Increasing Their Chance of Returning to the App

You fill out your profile, add a picture, and follow some of your friends. Maybe you post something or comment on someone else's post. Maybe you spend time scrolling on the app, hunting for the best videos or posts. That's all your "investment" into your experience on the app.

Now let's map this model to restaurants.

The Hook Canvas

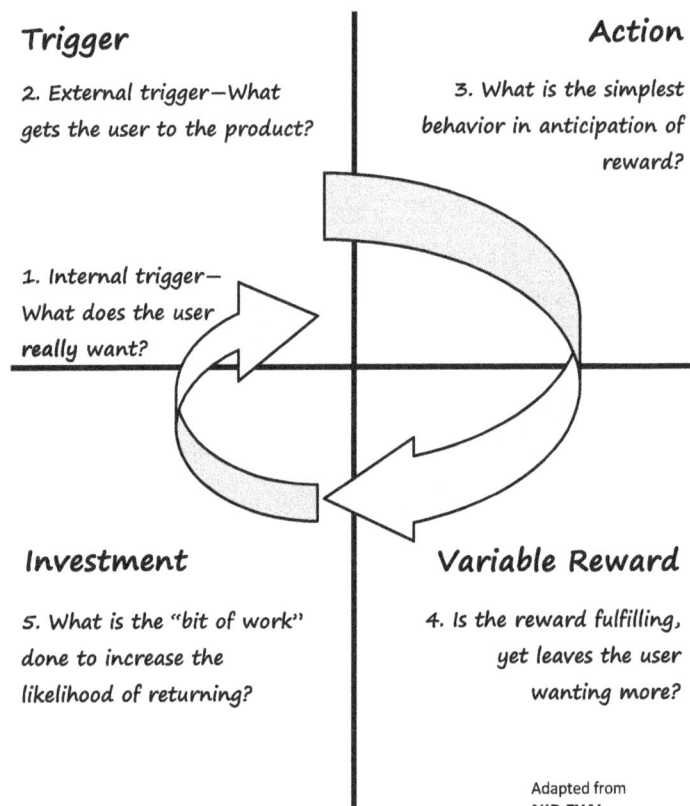

Trigger

2. External trigger—What gets the user to the product?

1. Internal trigger— What does the user really want?

Action

3. What is the simplest behavior in anticipation of reward?

Investment

5. What is the "bit of work" done to increase the likelihood of returning?

Variable Reward

4. Is the reward fulfilling, yet leaves the user wanting more?

Adapted from
NIR EYAL
NirAndFar.com
@nireyal

Part 1. Trigger: There are two kinds of triggers. The first is a craving for a certain dish or cuisine. Imagine Ellen googling "best pizza in Fort Worth." Her craving for pizza caused her to search for a type of restaurant. After she's eaten at your restaurant, the trigger changes. The trigger in the future might be, "It's Friday night, and I always order pizza for the family on Friday night." All restaurants have regulars who always order on the same day. Your automated marketing can send a reminder to order. For example, if Ellen tends to order from you on Tuesdays, your marketing system can automatically send her a reminder to order on Tuesdays. Her habit of ordering from you on Tuesdays is reinforced as she goes through the ordering cycle again and again.

Part 2. Action: When Ellen gives us her email address, that's an action. So is placing an order.

Part 3. Variable Reward: For restaurants, the variable reward is related to loyalty. After Ellen takes an action, we can show her the reward she's unlocked. Maybe it's a free lava cake. Maybe it's loyalty points that she can use to get free food later.

Part 4. Investment: The investment is the act of fielding the pickup or delivery order. If the food magically appeared beside Ellen (or someone else made the decision and ordered it), she would be less likely to reorder it in the future. Weird, right? Her habit is reinforced every time she goes through the process of selecting food, saving an order as her "favorite," tracking her order, and going to the front door when the food arrives.

CAMPAIGN 3: REGULAR REVIVAL

Next, imagine Ellen became a customer and then turned into a regular. She has ordered from you at least three times in the past three months. But some time has passed without her ordering.

At this point, the restaurant should flag Ellen as a "flight risk." The change in her ordering cadence means that this regular, whom you worked so hard to acquire, is at risk of drifting away.

When a regular is at risk, it's time to initiate the Regular Revival campaign.

That's when you quickly send a sequence of emails and text messages, spread out over some days, saying, "Hey, Ellen, we miss you. It's been two weeks since you last ordered from us, and we loved serving you your calzone. Click here to order now. Your calzone is waiting for you!"

This little nudge gets noticed.

If she doesn't respond to a friendly reminder via email or text, send her a tempting offer, like "Ellen, we really miss you. Here's free delivery on your next order so you can get your favorite calzone on Friday night."

The ideal "regular revival" messaging is hyper-personalized, financially appealing, and tied to a habit that she already created.

The goal is to ensure that Ellen doesn't go to one of your competitors or stop ordering from you completely.

In this campaign, you might send her up to five emails and text messages, each designed to keep her reordering.

This approach is key for keeping regulars engaged.

CAMPAIGN 4: REGULAR → WHALE

This last type of campaign is used to make more money from regulars.

The question here is "How can we turn a regular customer into a whale?"

For example, you've noticed that Ellen orders from you once a week now. You're sure Ellen is such a fan of the brand that she would love you to cater her next event.

So you send her an email about your catering program. You tell her she doesn't have to book you through ezCater.

You're transitioning her from a regular customer to a catering customer.

Now that she knows you offer catering, she comes to you with a $500 order for her office event. She spends ten times more than her typical $50 order, and this order has a higher profit margin too.

In another email, you might inform Ellen about your private events. What if she hosted her birthday party in your dining room? The email tells her it costs only $300 to rent your restaurant's entire back room. She and her friends and family can celebrate by eating her favorite food: calzones.

But imagine that you had never gotten Ellen's email address. Imagine she had floated away from your website, like 80 percent of visitors, and you had no way to get in touch with her. She probably never would have become a customer, let alone a regular.

Regulars like Ellen are the powerhouse of your business. Every restaurant needs these people. That's no secret.

The secret is that you can create regulars, just like you can create a customer out of a visitor. That's the power of marketing.

If you want step-by-step instructions and examples of how to set up these email campaigns, visit:

Owner.com/secret-emails

You now understand each part of the Restaurant Growth System. You can see how they all work together to drive sales. But I want you to know one last secret before you go.

This final secret can help you with your email marketing, website, app, and menu. This secret has been around for a long time. It has nothing to do with technology, yet it's more important than ever in our always-online world.

This last secret is about building a powerful brand.

Let's see how the leading restaurants do that.

Don't Serve Everyone

My friend Rahul Bhatia owns Saffron Indian Kitchen in Pennsylvania. It's a super successful, high-volume Indian restaurant that's been around for fifteen years.

When I first met him, he told me everybody in town loved his food. He said he just needed to create a web presence to attract more of "everybody"—young people, middle-aged people, old people. He saw all ages eat at Saffron from time to time. So he assumed that the entire community was his customer base.

Many restaurant owners feel this way, believing everyone should be their target since they have customers of all ages.

Everyone's gotta eat!

Restaurant Owner

Rahul's goal was to cast as wide a net as possible for the best return on marketing dollars.

This seemed like a good plan to me—at first.

We tried mass marketing for Rahul. (We were eager to use him as a case study to show the value of social media for a restaurant with broad appeal.)

We ran Facebook ads broadly targeting the people in Bala Cynwyd, Pennsylvania, but the resulting sales were pretty disappointing.

Then I decided to analyze his online ordering data.

I uploaded his customer list to a data enrichment platform for background checks, which gave me the ages and other facts about his customers.

Despite the diversity in his entire customer base, the top 20 percent—and especially the top 5 percent—of his customers had a specific profile: they were mostly moms between the ages of forty and sixty who lived in nearby suburbs and frequently ordered from Saffron for their families.

I reflected on why Rahul's biggest customers were these moms. And I realized that on a deep level, his restaurant celebrated family and togetherness.

His wife, Ruthie, was often in the dining room greeting customers. The menu appealed to families with its shareable, family-sized portions. The restaurant's decor included tablecloths and heirlooms that made visitors feel right at home. These details subconsciously communicated the message that this was a restaurant for people who value family.

It wasn't the eighteen-year-old frat bros from down the street at UPenn who were his top customers. It was people who saw parts of themselves in Rahul, Ruthie, and Saffron.

Without realizing it, Rahul had mastered branding by being specific about whom he served and what he wanted them to feel and creating an experience and story to achieve that.

Some restaurant owners say, "Everyone's gotta eat; my restaurant is for everyone!"

But that's the wrong way to think. We've found that when you try to be everything to everyone, you end up being nothing to anyone.

Instead, you want to be the first choice for the people who are looking for a restaurant just like yours.

Brands are to businesses what reputations are to people

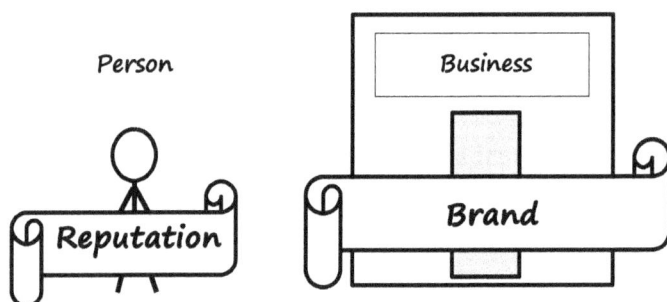

Becoming the first choice to those people involves having a great brand. Your brand is your reputation. With people, we call it a "reputation." With businesses, we call it a "brand."

My friends John Arena and Sam Facchini are brand masters. They own Metro Pizza in Las Vegas. They didn't set out to create a great brand. Neither of them has a marketing background. But they know their customers, inside and out.

John and Sam are constantly talking to their customers in the dining room. They know what their customers value. They know that their customers are usually between the ages of forty and sixty and that they value family.

John and Sam have designed everything about their messaging, their story, and their dining room to perfectly appeal to that group. Not to everyone. Just to that group.

It works. You'll see it if you walk into Metro Pizza, as I have done many times, and hang around with the owners. You'll see that people will come up to them to say hi.

Some customers have known John and Sam for fifteen or twenty years.

Sometimes it's been years since they've talked. But it feels like just yesterday.

Thousands of Metro Pizza customers know the owners' names. They know their whole story. It's because Sam and John have done such a masterful job of becoming legendary to these people, in this area.

Sam and John show the long-term effect of having a great brand. Spending $50,000 on Facebook ads focused on your city—that will drive some orders to your restaurant. It might even drive enough orders to make back more than $50,000 in sales.

But there's a hidden price tag when you run those Facebook ads.

Almost always, you're offering some ridiculous deal, like 50 percent off a customer's first order. The vast majority of those customers aren't going to order from you again and again. They're not going to value your food very much; they associate it with the discount.

But when a customer comes to you because they can feel that your brand perfectly meets their needs—it gives them a place they can go to with their family when they're craving pizza, a place that reflects their identity and values—you don't just get one order. You get that customer for life.

Over the course of ten, twenty, or thirty years, that customer could order from you every week. They could easily spend tens of thousands of dollars, and even hundreds of thousands of dollars, with you. (It seems unreal, but this is a pattern I've noticed with all restaurants. A tiny fraction of customers, the "whales," bring the vast majority of profits over time.)

So there's a huge long-term benefit to playing the long game with your brand. We see the benefit in the businesses that have aced branding for decades.

Some people, like John and Sam, have aced it almost by accident, without really thinking about it.

But don't worry; there's a way to do it on purpose. So how do you develop a great brand?

All the restaurants we've seen that have great brands do three things:

1. They identify their ideal customer.
2. They decide how they want the customers to feel about their restaurant.
3. They tell a story that makes customers feel that way.

Let's talk through each of these elements.

STEP 1: IDENTIFY YOUR IDEAL CUSTOMER

I used to think the best way for a restaurant to make money was to have a brand that appealed to everyone. That way, when you marketed your food, as many people as possible would be interested.

But I was wrong. The best restaurants appeal to specific groups and narrow their ideal or target customer. They all tend to appeal to a specific group—even if it's not immediately obvious—and repel others.

For example, everybody likes pizza. When most people think of pizza, the first brand they think of is Domino's because it's the global leader in pizza.

Yet Domino's doesn't appeal to everybody. If I called my sixty-year-old mom right now and asked her about Domino's, I can already hear what she would say: "Yuck! It's disgusting. It tastes like cardboard."

Almost everybody in her age group has that same opinion.

But if I walked down the street to the college near me and asked the twenty-year-old guys what they think about Domino's, they'd say, "Domino's is the best!"

That's because the ideal Domino's customer is a young man between the ages of twenty and thirty. Financially, Domino's customers tend to be low-earning. Data shows that typical Domino's customers, contrary to popular belief, are just as specific as Rahul's customers in terms of lifestyle, age, and gender.

That's not by accident. While I was researching for this book, I learned a fact that made my jaw drop.

Tom Monaghan, the founder of Domino's, was twenty-three years old when he started the company.

Is it a coincidence that he chose an ideal customer just like him—a low-earning man between the ages of twenty and thirty?

I don't think so.

Tom was the person he was trying to serve, so he was able to predict customers' tastes. He could quickly create an experience that appealed to them.

Every decision the company has made since then has been designed to appeal to their target customer.

That doesn't mean that older women never order Domino's—exceptions do exist. But almost all of Domino's most frequent customers are young men between the ages of twenty and thirty. And how do you think the corporate leaders at Domino's decide where to open new locations? They decide based on which neighborhoods have the most young men.

Once you define your ideal customer, you can use that to inform your business decisions. That includes your menu, design, locations, pricing, marketing taglines, and more. So the first step is deciding whom you want to build your reputation with. Because that's what a brand is: the reputation of your restaurant.

Once you know who your perfect customer is, it's time to get clear on what you want them to feel when they think of your brand.

STEP 2: DECIDE HOW YOU WANT PEOPLE TO FEEL WHEN THEY THINK ABOUT YOUR RESTAURANT

How should people feel when they think about your restaurant? The right answer depends on the needs of your ideal customer. Different groups of customers have different needs.

Let's go back to Domino's. We now know that Domino's focuses on young men in the lower-middle class.

The next question Domino's had to answer in planning their brand was, "How do we want to make those young men feel when they think of Domino's?"

Well, young men are known to be pretty impatient, and they do things at the last minute. They tend to be on a tight budget. So what did Domino's build their brand around? Convenience, speed, and low cost.

Domino's is trying to make customers feel relief. Relief from hunger. Relief that tasty food is on the way as fast as humanly possible and at a cheap price. And even some excitement about the ability to get a Supreme Pizza and Chocolate Lava Crunch

Cake in less than thirty minutes. Excitement and relief are two of the emotions Domino's is going for.

The ideal Domino's customer doesn't care much about the quality or healthiness of the food, so Domino's is not going for quality or trying to be known as healthy. That's why the groups of people who care more about that, like my mom, are so disgusted by the brand.

The brand feeling of Domino's doesn't end there.

Domino's meets young men's practical needs by being the fastest and cheapest option. But that doesn't meet the most important emotional need that a restaurant brand should satisfy.

The most successful restaurant brands also make their customers feel a sense of belonging. They ensure their ideal customers feel at home with their restaurant. They get their customers to think, "This is for people like me." Restaurants achieve that through the third step: telling a story that makes the customers feel those emotions. And the way Domino's does it is absolutely genius.

STEP 3: TELL THE STORY THAT MAKES THEM FEEL THOSE EMOTIONS

When I say story, I don't mean a story like "Once upon a time, a young girl named Little Red Riding Hood went to visit her grandmother in the woods."

In branding, the story consists of the details that a company uses to make the ideal customer feel a certain way about the restaurant.

Once you identify who your customer is and what emotions you want them to feel, you can develop creative messaging, details, and storytelling to make them feel those emotions. Building a relationship with loyal customers starts with the stories you tell around your brand. That includes your founding story and mission. Then the story is reinforced by the little decisions we make to shape the brand.

In Domino's case, the founding story is that Tom Monaghan bought the original Domino's for $900.

At the time, it was a small pizzeria called DomiNick's.

Tom transformed it into Domino's, inspired by a game that he thought was edgy and cool.

By being entrepreneurial, he grew it and grew it and grew it over the years.

It's the perfect story for his ideal customer! Many young men at that age are also trying to make something of their lives through entrepreneurship and hard work.

That's the story Domino's used to make other young men feel like they belong. It's a story of being a brand for young men, by young men.

But the founding story is just one part of the larger story of Domino's.

For example, for the first few decades of growing their brand, Domino's told a story about their thirty-minute guarantee. It's so famous that you still hear people talk about it now, more than twenty years after those commercials stopped.

In that story, Domino's used its marketing to tell customers that if they didn't get their delivery in thirty minutes, it was free. What better way to make them feel like they could count on the brand for fast relief from hunger?

That was a story that grabbed attention and made customers think of Domino's as the fastest option.

The other major story they told in their marketing was about their great deals. In 2005, they spent millions of dollars on a commercial with Donald Trump featuring what they called their "5-5-5 deal." They had a Domino's driver deliver a pizza to Donald Trump in his golden penthouse.

As the driver walks up to the penthouse door, he says to Donald Trump, "Here you go; three medium pizzas, five dollars each."

Trump pauses, looks at the driver, and makes a counteroffer, looking all smart.

"Tell you what," Trump says. "I'll counter that offer with an even better one. Here's the deal. You give me those three pizzas, and I'll give you just five dollars for each of them."

Domino's deal couldn't be beat—not even by Trump!

This was another genius form of marketing because it told a story to reinforce the trait Domino's wanted to be known for: great value. To get attention for that story, Domino's used Donald Trump, who was especially loved by young men.

By the way, storytelling doesn't have to just be commercials. Storytelling in restaurant branding can be any detail of the restaurant's execution, like what language the menu is written in.

For example, some of Domino's top-selling items are the Cheeseburger Pizza and the ExtravaganZZa Feast Pizza. Their most popular dessert is called the Chocolate Lava Crunch Cake.

Are these names that would appeal to people like my sixty-year-old mom?

Hell no! Absolutely not.

But they're the perfect names to reinforce the story that this brand is for young men.

A few years ago, Domino's made another major decision: to go all-in on technology. These days, they call themselves a technology company that happens to sell pizza.

Whom does that story resonate with? Who thinks technology is cool? Again, it's those young men.

Would you like a cheeseburger pizza?

Yuck!

Restaurant Server

Mom

Each of these details fits the reputation that Domino's wants to have.

Domino's visual identity also reinforces their story. Their main logo color is bright blue—a very masculine color. And the Domino's secondary logo color is race car red—also masculine.

But it doesn't end there. During the 1960s, dominos was one of the most popular gambling games for young men and also a popular toy among young boys. So Tom decided Domino's was the perfect name. He wanted his customers to associate his pizza brand with fun, games, and friends.

Having decided whom he wanted to serve, Tom created the perfect set of symbols that appealed to those young men. It made them feel like they were at home in his restaurant, with his brand. It made them think, "This looks like it's for me."

SMALL BUSINESSES CAN DO THIS

Now you've seen how the whole three-step framework comes together with Domino's:

1. *Who's the ideal customer?* Young men.
2. *How should they feel when they think about the restaurant?* The main feeling is relief, from hunger and from financial stress (since the food is cheap). The other feelings are "fun, playful, and homey." Customers should associate Domino's with having fun, playing games with friends, and feeling at home.
3. *What's the story that makes them feel that way?* Everything about Domino's tells its brand story: the logo, the colors, the name, the menu items, the technology, and the founding story.

```
Restaurant

Domino's

Who's the ideal customer?

Young men

How should they feel when they
think about the restaurant?

Relief from hunger
Relief from financial stress
Fun
Playful
Comfortable like home

What's the story that makes them
feel that way?

Domino's is a tech company that happens to
sell pizza. It's inexpensive. It has fun items on
its menu like cheeseburger pizza. And its logo
and colors reinforce that its branding is fun
and masculine.
```

You don't have to be Domino's to have great branding. I have seen single-location restaurants make millions of dollars by perfecting their branding.

We'll start with an example of a restaurant that's the exact opposite of Domino's, yet is still wildly successful.

That example is Ottavio's Italian Restaurant in Lakeside, California, made successful by Antoinette Belvedere.

Antoinette knows her customers well. There's a retirement home right down the street from her, and the neighborhood is composed mainly of older people. That means her ideal customer is between the ages of sixty-five and eighty, upper middle class, and equally likely to be a man or a woman. So Step 1 is easy for Antoinette.

Step 2 is how she wants her ideal customer to feel when they think about her brand, Ottavio's.

Upper-middle-class retirees in that age group tend to care about two things: family and community. So Antoinette wanted to make her customers feel connected to their community. They should feel that every order is a way to support people with similar values.

Antoinette nailed Step 3: telling her brand story through the details. Everything about her restaurant experience lovingly tells the story of family and community.

The Ottavio's logo is a picture of her grandfather (who started the restaurant). She uses that image to tell guests the founding story of her restaurant. It's the story of her family.

The story tells how her grandpa emigrated from Italy and brought his family's recipes to the States. And now the family's tradition is serving the people in their community of Lakeside.

Restaurant

Ottavio's

Who's the ideal customer?

Upper-middle-class men and women ages 65+

How should they feel when they think about the restaurant?

They should feel like they're supporting people who care about family and community.

What's the story that makes them feel that way?

Ottavio's is a family restaurant started by Antoinette's grandfather who emigrated from Italy. It serves family recipes to the community of Lakeside. Its logo and colors are warm and festive—perfect for a family gathering.

This branding is how Ottavio's has grown a cult-like following. It's how they're doing millions of dollars in sales with just one small location.

The brand story perfectly fits the needs of Antoinette's customers. It especially meets their emotional needs. It creates a reputation that makes those people feel like this restaurant is for people like them.

Every other detail of her restaurant strengthens that story.

Her dining room looks like a family's dining room. It has a cozy, loving feel.

Antoinette chose red, gold, and white as colors for her brand. They're warm, festive colors that are perfect for a family occasion.

She offers menu items that her customers associate with family, like baked rigatoni lasagna. She describes it on the menu as her family's recipe from Italy.

Creating this brand allows Antoinette to charge more. Like Domino's, Ottavio's has a twelve-inch pizza—but Ottavio's charges 20 percent to 50 percent more.

Domino's 12-inch pizza   **Ottavio's 12-inch pizza**

$12   **$18**

And her customers happily pay. They buy pizza from her even though there's a Domino's right down the street that's faster and cheaper.

Why? Because the brand details make customers feel like Ottavio's is of higher quality. And it's for people who care about quality—people like them. It gives them that sense of belonging. It makes them feel that the brand aligns with their values and identity.

One major advantage that single-location restaurants have over chains is the ultimate detail to reinforce the story: the owner is there. People meet Antoinette and her father, Lenny, in the restaurant. They get to know each other as people. When people know the owner of a restaurant, they become cultlike in their loyalty, and word of mouth about the restaurant spreads.

Would Antoinette be as successful with the same brand and prices in a college town? Definitely not, because there would be a mismatch. She'd have to build a different brand or move somewhere else.

PROOF THAT THIS SECRET IS WORTH BILLIONS

I have one more example for you that really brings home the point Don't Serve Everyone.

It's a great example because it's one of the most successful restaurants founded in the past twenty years.

The brand is called Cava. The CEO, Brett Schulman, is a branding genius.

Cava became a public company recently—it's being traded on the stock exchange. It was worth $4 billion last I checked. It's a Mediterranean chain that specializes in hummus and rice bowls.

On the surface, you'd think, "Well, anybody should be able to like healthy bowls with hummus and rice."

But we know better. That's not the approach Cava takes.

Instead, they know exactly who their ideal customer is. They answer the question from Step 1—"Who is my ideal customer?"—very specifically. It's women in their thirties and forties who are upper middle class.

Women in that group tend to care about health and taking care of people. So Cava tells a brand story that's all about health and taking care of the community.

Now that we know the ideal customer, let's focus on the question from Step 2: "How do we want to make them feel?" Cava first wants to make customers feel like they belong at Cava. They also want to make them feel comforted and validated. They want their customers to feel like this brand shares their values and understands the type of person they are.

Time for Step 3: tell a story that makes the customers feel those things.

In multiple places on Cava's website, they say it's their mission to help people "eat well and live well."

The website also says that Cava is all about "taking care of people and the things that feed us." They want us to know that they take care of the earth, farmers, and their team.

This is the perfect message for an upper-middle-class woman in her thirties or forties because she tends to care about most of those things. But what if we showed that same message to the ideal twenty-year-old Domino's customer? It wouldn't be a fit.

Restaurant

Cava

Who's the ideal customer?

Upper-middle-class women in their 30s–40s

How should they feel when they think about the restaurant?

They should feel like Cava shares their values and understands that they're health-conscious people who care for others.

What's the story that makes them feel that way?

Cava's mission is to help people eat well and live well. Cava is all about taking care of people and the things that feed us: the earth, farmers, and the Cava team.

To Cava's ideal customer, the story of a brand that is about eating well and taking care of people is very attractive. But Cava's success doesn't end with the brand story. That's where it starts. All the details of Cava rhyme with that story.

On their website, every picture is designed to say to those high-earning women, "This is for you."

Scrolling through the site while researching for this book, I noticed that every major food picture included a woman's hand holding a bowl, her beautiful nails painted perfectly.

Most men probably wouldn't notice this. But I bet women would.

That elegant hand with the fresh forty-dollar manicure says to them, "This restaurant is for people like us. We feel like we belong here."

Cava has made a lot of its business details public. And it turns out that their internal numbers reflect their success in marketing to their target customer. They even choose to open new locations in cities that have especially high populations of upper-middle-class women in their thirties and forties.

Now that you know this secret, you can see it everywhere. You can see it with Nobu, for example. They know their demographic is sophisticated, wealthy people in their fifties. That explains the language they use to describe each item on their menu and the decisions they make about what dishes to put on the menu.

According to Nobu's website right now, their dishes are "meticulously crafted" with "subtle nuance." Their chefs have perfected "the symphony of timing."

What do those words make you feel?

The brand seems ritzy and highbrow. The language is so complicated that some people might not understand it. Nobu knows exactly who their target audience is.

One last big-picture point to make here is that the brand story has to be consistent. That's a huge part of what makes people believe it.

Many brands lately have even made customers angry by being inconsistent. They may suddenly claim to be eco-friendly or serve healthy food.

For example, maybe a decade ago, McDonald's added a bunch of salads to their menu. Out of nowhere, they started saying they were green and healthy. But nobody believed them. The reason is that the rest of McDonald's story contradicts their claim of being green and healthy.

They were met with backlash. Soon, salads were back off their menu.

Just as people don't buy salads from McDonald's, they also don't buy the messaging around McDonald's "healthy" food. So it doesn't help their brand to include that stuff.

When you're clear about whom you serve and what you want them to feel, you can avoid those mistakes.

You can ensure that all the different parts of the customer experience reinforce that story.

You can make sure none of them are in conflict.

This consistency leads to an honest, believable brand that people can trust.

If you want step-by-step instructions and examples of how to do this for your restaurant, visit:

Owner.com/secret-branding

The Good News

Right now you might feel like Neo from *The Matrix*. When he first saw the world as it truly is, it was intimidating. He was almost too scared to face the problem.

You're not alone. The content I've created on these topics gets hundreds of thousands of views every month. People across the industry are hungry for solutions to these challenging problems.

But now that you see the reality, you have an obligation to yourself and your business to take the necessary steps to succeed online. In this book, we've covered the strategies and the system for doing that.

The good news is that you're now ahead of 99 percent of restaurant owners because you have the system. You can see how everything needs to be connected to drive sales.

Restaurant Growth System

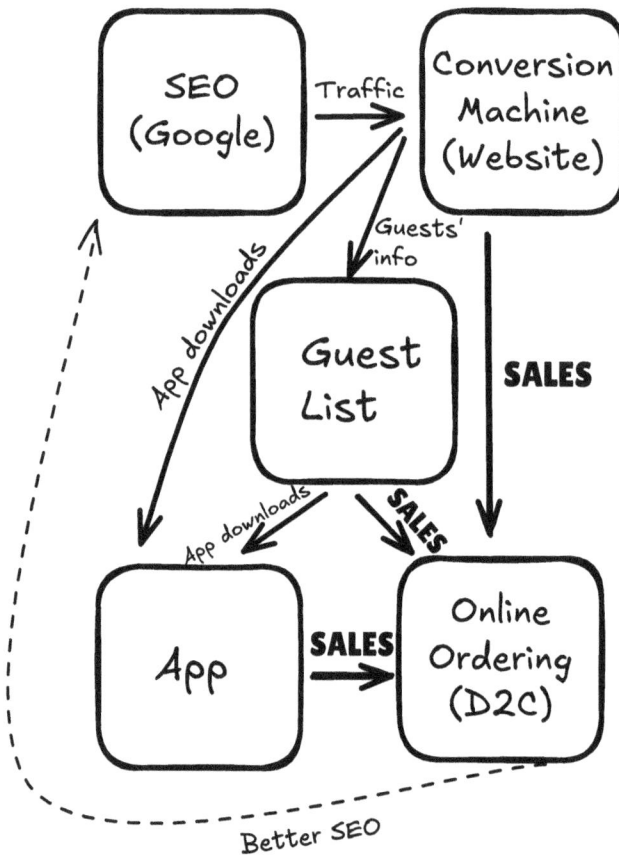

You've identified the major secrets of the industry. You know the ways you've been misled.

Now you have a strategic understanding of how to elevate your business.

At the big-picture level, you understand what to do.

The next step is to start executing. You can follow our guides, which walk you through building a successful restaurant online step by step. The guides are free. You can check them out here:

Owner.com/secret-guides

I suggest starting with the guides on acquiring new customers with SEO. Then move on to maximizing the value of each customer. We make it easy, with no need for you to buy any software. We outline what works and provide everything you need to act on what you've learned.

The hopeful news is that I've seen thousands of restaurants, from various backgrounds and even on the brink of bankruptcy, use this playbook to save or improve their business.

More good news is that most people want to see you succeed. That includes people in your community.

Independent restaurants add uniqueness and character to neighborhoods. They're places of joy and gathering. No one wants to see a trend of chain restaurants like Applebee's taking over while beloved local spots close down.

The strategies in this book will help those who already love your restaurant to buy more easily and more frequently. They'll celebrate your success, and they'll support you as you transition.

They'll understand you better through storytelling, and they'll know they can get a great experience ordering directly from you.

A world without independent restaurants would lack color. It would be a world of corporate sameness, devoid of the unique aspects of neighborhoods that people are proud to call home.

The world needs your restaurant.